AFFIRMATIVE ACTION

Point/Counterpoint

Philosophers Debate Contemporary Issues
General Editors: James P. Sterba and Rosemarie Tong

This new series will provide a philosophical angle to debates currently raging in academic and larger circles. Each book will be a short volume (around 200 pages) in which two prominent philosophers debate different sides of an issue. Future topics might include the canon, the ethics of abortion rights, and the death penalty. For more information contact Professor Sterba, Department of Philosophy, University of Notre Dame, Notre Dame, IN 46566, or Professor Tong, Department of Philosophy, Davidson College, Davidson, NC 28036.

Political Correctness: For and Against
>Marilyn Friedman, Washington University, St. Louis
>Jan Narveson, University of Waterloo, Ontario, Canada

Humanitarian Intervention: Just War vs. Pacifism
>Robert L. Phillips, University of Connecticut
>Duane L. Cady, Hamline University

Affirmative Action: Social Justice or Unfair Preference?
>Albert G. Mosley, Ohio University
>Nicholas Capaldi, University of Tulsa

AFFIRMATIVE ACTION

Social Justice or Unfair Preference?

Albert G. Mosley
and
Nicholas Capaldi

ROWMAN & LITTLEFIELD PUBLISHERS, INC.
Lanham • Boulder • New York • London

ROWMAN & LITTLEFIELD PUBLISHERS, INC.

Published in the United States of America
by Rowman & Littlefield Publishers, Inc.
4720 Boston Way, Lanham, Maryland 20706

3 Henrietta Street
London WC2E 8LU, England

British Cataloging in Publication Information Available

Library of Congress Cataloging-in-Publication Data
Mosley, Albert G.
    Affirmative action : social justice or unfair preference? / Albert
G. Mosley and Nicholas Capaldi.
    p. cm. — (Point/Counterpoint)
    Includes bibliographical references and index.
    ISBN 0-8476-8301-X (cloth : alk. paper). — ISBN 0-8476-8302-8
(pbk. : alk. paper)
    1. Affirmative action programs—Law and legislation—United
States. 2. Affirmative action programs—United States. 3. Reverse
discrimination in employment—United States. I. Capaldi, Nicholas.
II. Title. III. Series.
KF3464.M67   1996
342.73'0873—dc20
[347.302873] 96-28097   CIP

ISBN 0–8476–8301–X (cloth : alk. paper)
ISBN 0–8476–8302–8 (pbk : alk. paper)

Printed in the United States of America

∞ ™ The paper used in this publication meets the minimum requirements
of American National Standard for Information Sciences—Permanence of
Paper for Printed Library Materials, ANSI Z39.48–1984.

Contents

Preface

Affirmative action has been a controversial policy, especially within the academic world, since its inception about three decades ago. Recently it has become a central issue in the presidential campaign and in various states as well as numerous court cases. Our joint aim has been to convey some sense of the history and meaning of this controversy. The issues we discuss lie at the heart of any conception of what the American experience has meant and can continue to mean. We believe that students, teachers, those connected with the law and public policy, and the intelligent lay public will all benefit from this discussion.

As befits the nature of the Point/Counterpoint series, we have tried to illuminate the issues by taking opposing sides and accentuating our differences. At the same time our approach is philosophical in attempting to identify and articulate the fundamental presuppositions of the debate and the arguments that can be offered in support of and opposition to those presuppositions. We begin with independently written essays and follow this with rebuttals of each other's position. We did not negotiate over what was or was not a fair and reasonable interpretation of our work, nor did we attempt to alter one another's response. We pulled no punches, for it is our firm joint conviction that the truth will best emerge in the mind of the reader who is presented with tough work through the arguments. The commitment on the part of both authors is pedagogical not antagonistic, that is we hope to illuminate the issues not win the argument.

We jointly thank James Sterba and Rosemarie Tong, the editors of the series, for inviting us to participate and for aiding us in the exchange of views. We also thank Jennifer Ruark, Acquisitions Editor for Rowman & Littlefield, for her orchestration of the final product. Professor Capaldi adds additional thanks to his wife Nadia for her patience in illuminating the law, to William Allen for calling attention to the wider public policy dimensions of the debate, to Steven Chesser his research assistant, and to the staff of the Intercollegiate Studies Institute for calling attention to material that might otherwise have been missed. Professor Mosley would also like to thank his wife Kathleen for her support and many references, his research assistant Samuel Hunter, Jr. for exceptional service and discussions, the Ohio University Research Council for research funding, my colleagues James Petrik, Richard Manning, Bob Trevis, Peter Kousaleos, and Bill Smith for reading and commenting on earlier drafts, and a very special thanks to my department chair Donald Borchert for his efforts and support.

The strengths of these essays owe much to these people; the weaknesses, no doubt, to our reluctance always to follow their advice. The authors accept full responsibility for the views expressed.

Affirmative Action: Pro

Albert G. Mosley

Legislative and Judicial Background

In 1941, Franklin Roosevelt issued Executive Order 8802 banning discrimination in employment by the federal government and defense contractors. Subsequently, many bills were introduced in Congress mandating equal employment opportunity but none were passed until the Civil Rights Act of 1964. The penalty for discrimination in Executive Order 8802 and the bills subsequently proposed was that the specific victim of discrimination be "made whole," that is, put in the position he or she would have held were it not for the discriminatory act, including damages for lost pay and legal expenses.

The contemporary debate concerning affirmative action can be traced to the landmark decision of *Brown v. Board of Education* (1954), whereby local, state, and federal ordinances enforcing segregation by race were ruled unconstitutional. In subsequent opinions, the Court ruled that state-mandated segregation in libraries, swimming pools, and other publicly funded facilities was also unconstitutional. In *Swann v. Charlotte-Mecklenburg* (1971), the Court declared that "in order to prepare students to live in a pluralistic society" school authorities might implement their desegregation order by deciding that "each school should have a prescribed ratio of Negro to White students reflecting the proportion for the district as a whole."[1] The ratio was not to be an inflexible one, but should reflect local variations in the ratio of Whites to Blacks. But any predominantly one-race school in a district with a mixed population and a history of segregation was subject to "close scrutiny." This requirement was attacked by conservatives as imposing a "racial quota," a charge that reverberates in the contemporary debate concerning affirmative action.

With the Montgomery bus boycotts of the mid-1950s, Blacks initiated an era of nonviolent direct action to publicly protest unjust laws and practices that supported racial discrimination. The graphic portrayals of repression and violence produced by the civil rights movement precipitated a national revulsion against the unequal treatment of African Americans. Blacks demanded their constitutional right to participate in the political process and share equal access to public accommodations, government-supported programs, and employment opportunities. But as John F. Kennedy stated in an address to Congress: "There is little value in a Negro's obtaining the right to be admitted to hotels and restaurants if he has no cash in his pocket and no job."[2]

Kennedy stressed that the issue was not merely eliminating discrimination, but eliminating as well the oppressive economic and social burdens imposed on Blacks by racial discrimination.[3] To this end, he advocated a weak form of affirmative action, involving eliminating discrimination and expanding educational and employment opportunities (including apprenticeships and on-the-job training). The liberal vision was that, given such opportunities, Blacks would move up the economic ladder to a degree relative to their own merit. Thus, a principal aim of the Civil Rights Act of 1964 was to effect a redistribution of social, political, and economic benefits and to provide legal remedies for the denial of individual rights.

The Civil Rights Act of 1964

The first use of the phrase "affirmative action" is found in Executive Order 10952, issued by President John F. Kennedy in 1961. This order established the Equal Employment Opportunity Commission (EEOC) and directed that contractors on projects funded, in whole or in part, with federal funds "take affirmative action to ensure that applicants are employed, and employees are treated during their employment, without regard to the race, creed, color, or national origin."

As a result of continuing public outrage at the level of violence and animosity shown toward Blacks, a stronger version of the Civil Rights

Bill was presented to the Congress than Kennedy had originally recommended. Advocates pointed out that Blacks suffered an unemployment rate that was twice that of Whites and that Black employment was concentrated in semiskilled and unskilled jobs. They emphasized that national prosperity would be improved by eliminating discrimination and integrating Black talent into its skilled and professional workforce.[4]

Fewer Blacks were employed in professional positions than had the requisite skills, and those Blacks who did occupy positions commensurate with their skill level had half the lifetime earnings of Whites. Such facts were introduced during legislative hearings to show the need to more fully utilize and reward qualified Blacks throughout the labor force, and not merely in the unskilled and semiskilled sectors.

While the bill was being debated, there was intense pressure from civil rights supporters that a stronger version of the bill be passed, which would have empowered the Department of Justice to pursue systemic as well as individual cases of discrimination. Advocates of a stronger bill stressed the grossly unequal distribution of economic benefits (double unemployment among Blacks, average lifetime income of Black college graduates less than that of eighth-grade White dropouts), but they did not advocate proportional representation or racial balance. Rather, Senator Hubert Humphrey argued that "the goal was to see to it that people were employed on the basis of merit rather than on false standards such as color or race."[5]

In opposition, southern senators such as Senators Sam Ervin (D-S.C.) and John Sparkman (D-Ala.) argued that the bill extended the power of the federal government by denying Americans their basic economic, personal, and property rights, for the sole benefit of the Black segment of the population.[6] A minority report in the House of Representatives by representatives from Louisiana, Georgia, Virginia, South Carolina, North Carolina, and Missisippi argued that the rights of employers to hire and fire, the rights of unions to choose members, the rights of postsecondary and professional schools to choose students, and seniority rights in employment would be egregiously impaired by the proposed Civil Rights Act.[7] Senator Ervin's amendment to delete Title VII from the Civil Rights Bill was defeated. But the question of whether emphasis should be on prosecuting individual cases of discrimination or eliminating broad discriminatory practices remained unresolved. Nonetheless, the clear intent of Title VI and Title VII of the bill was to eliminate discrimination and redistribute opportunities so that Blacks were not limited to the lower end of the educational and employment spectrum.

In 1965 President Lyndon Johnson issued Executive Order 11246, which gave the Department of Labor primary responsibility for enforcing affirmative action. To this end, the Labor Department established the Office of Federal Contract Compliance and took the proactive stance that contractors to the federal government must show that, prior to the award of government contracts, they had proactive plans to ensure the inclusion of minorities in their workforce. Labor union leadership gave lip service to antidiscrimination efforts, but local unions (especially of the AFL) were rigidly segregated and rabidly opposed to the inclusionary role of affirmative action.

1972 Amendments to the Civil Rights Act

The U.S. Commission on Civil Rights was empowered to monitor the efforts of enforcement agencies, and in 1971 the commission provided comprehensive evidence that meaningful results were not being produced. Subsequently, Congress passed the Equal Employment Opportunity Act of 1972 extending the Equal Employment Opportunity Commission's (EEOC) oversight to employers and unions with over fifteen members and to all state, local, and federal government employees. A council was established to coordinate the activities of the various agencies involved in enforcement of Title VII, and the EEOC was granted enforcement powers and jurisdiction over cases involving institutional patterns of exclusion.

A primary justification of the 1972 bill was the realization that the enforcement machinery necessary to ensure the redistributive goals of the Civil Rights Act was woefully inadequate. The 1972 bill also gave greater recognition to systemic discrimination rather than the traditional focus on individual cases. Allowing class action suits recognized that some cases of discrimination extended further than the particular individuals instituting the suit and, hence, that each individual entitled to relief need not be named in the claim for relief.[8]

In 1970, under President Nixon and then secretary of labor George Shultz, the federal government instituted the Philadelphia Plan, requiring that the highly segregated construction contractors and labor unions of Philadelphia employ more minority workers. The plan was extended in Order no.4, issued by the Labor Department, according to which employers with at least fifty employees and $50,000 in government business were to develop "specific goals and timetables" to correct for the underutilization of minority workers. A firm, informed of its noncompliance with the affirmative action guidelines, had 120 days in which to present the Office of Federal Contract Compliance Programs (OFCCP) with a plan to correct its underutilization, or face the loss of government business.

In 1971, the Labor Department issued Revised Order No.4, which had been extended to include women as well as minority workers. Major corporations (Bethlehem Steel, AT&T) and universities (Columbia University) were forced to end discriminatory practices and initiate affirmative action plans to employ and promote more women and minorities. In the same year, the Supreme Court interpreted Title VII to proscribe "not only overt discrimination but also processes that are fair in form but discriminatory in operation."[9]

The Department of Health, Education, and Welfare also issued guidelines to implement Title VI of the Civil Rights Act, which prohibited discrimination on the basis of race, color, or national origin in the distribution of benefits in any federally assisted programs. Recipients of federal funds were required to "take affirmative action to overcome the effects of prior discrimination" and "even in the absence of such prior discrimination, a recipient in administering a program may take affirmative action to overcome the effects of conditions which resulted in limiting participation of a particular race, color, or national origin." To illustrate, "where a university is not adequately serving members of a particular racial or nationality group, it may establish special recruitment policies to make its program better known and more readily available to such group, and take other steps to provide that group with more adequate service."[10]

Constitutional challenges to affirmative action have been based primarily on the Equal Protection Clause of the Fourteenth Amendment, which prohibits state and local governments from denying a person within their jurisdictions the equal protection of the law. Moreover, the Supreme Court has held that classifications that involve fundamental rights (e.g., political activity, freedom of movement, right to privacy) or minorities (race, national origins) are subject to *strict scrutiny*. This means that such classifications must be used in the service of a compelling government interest, be narrowly tailored to that interest, and be necessary for the achievement of that interest. These requirements are designed to discourage the use of suspect classifications, and few policies survive such review.

Intermediate scrutiny, on the other hand, requires only that the use of a classification serve important (rather than compelling) governmental interests and that it be rationally related to (rather than necessary for) the achievement of those interests.

Using race as a means of increasing the access of Blacks to political, educational, and economic opportunities would be a benign classification given the history of racism in America. On the other hand, using race as a means of excluding Blacks or Whites from such opportunities would be invidious. However, whether the Fourteenth Amendment to the Constitution and the Civil rights Act of 1964 forbids both invidious and benign uses of race in the design of public policies has been a point of contention. In some cases, the courts have held that the government (e.g., in *Fullilove v. Klutznich, Metro Broadcasting Inc. v. F.C.C.*) and private agencies (e.g., in *United Steelworkers v. Weber*) may use race in crafting policies to remedy past discrimination and increase diversity. In more recent decisions, however, the Court has held even benign uses to the more stringent criteria of strict scrutiny (*City of Richmond v. Croson, Adarand Constructors v. Pena*).

Title VII explicitly prohibits the use of race, color, religion, sex, or national origin by employers (of at least fifteen people), employment agencies, and labor organizations to exclude individuals from the full benefits offered by those agencies unless such use serves a bona fide occupational qualification. It also prohibits employment practices that perpetuate the effects of past discrimination, except where such is the result of a bona fide seniority or merit system. Moreover, section 703j explicitly denies that Title VII requires preferential treatment or a racial balance.

Title VII did not specify the definition of discrimination, and the courts have distinguished three forms it may take: (1) *disparate treatment*, classifying people as different who are similar in the relevant respects or classifying people as similar who are different in the relevant respects; (2) *adverse impact*, when a seemingly neutral procedure such as testing, interviewing, or educational requirements disproportionately eliminates a particular group from certain opportunities without those procedures being relevant to fulfilling the requirements of that opportunity; and (3) *perpetuating the effects of past discrimination into the present*, as when an agreement between management and union effectively excludes a particular group from training, promotion, and retention benefits.

Adverse impact might indicate discrimination even though the discriminatory effect was produced by "practices, procedures, or tests neutral on their face, and even neutral in terms of intent" but which were not necessary for the proper performance of the position in question.[11] Adverse impact occurs when a practice produces an underrepresentation of a race, sex, or ethnic group in a given workforce. According to the 1978 Uniform Guidelines on Employee Selection Procedures (for compliance with Revised Order No. 4 of the Carter administration), a practice has an adverse impact on a group if it resulted in a selection rate from that group that was less than four-fifths the selection rate of the group with the highest selection rate.[12] Where there is a pattern of exclusion, the remedy seeks to correct the resulting underrepresentation through special recruitment efforts, goals, and timetables, and, in the most egregious cases, strict numerical quotas until a certain level of representation is reached.[13]

Thus, as in *Griggs v. Duke Power Co.* (1971), requiring a high school diploma or passing score on an intelligence test for jobs that could be performed without need of such would disproportinately affect Blacks and other groups who historically had been denied equal educational benefits. Such "color-blind" qualifications would also exclude many Whites from jobs for which they would otherwise qualify. By outlawing irrelevant requirements and recruitment based on personal networks, affirmative action has made it possible for more people in general to have opportunities that otherwise would have been reserved for a privileged few.[14] This has led Derrick Bell to argue that, contrary to popular opinion, marginalized Whites (women and less well-connected males) have benefited more from affirmative action than Blacks.[15]

Illegal discrimination would also be indicated in practices that perpetuate the effects of past discrimination into the present. Title VII explicitly excluded bona fide seniority systems from this category. On the other hand, the Court held that other practices (e.g., collective bargaining agreements that locked Blacks into lower paying job categories) were not excluded.[16] Agreements requiring union apprenticeships for certain jobs, where Blacks had been denied union membership, reinforced and perpetuated the effects of past discrimination, even if the agreements were not instituted with the intent of adversely affecting Blacks.

Remedies required by a finding of discrimination included hiring, reinstatement, backpay, retroactive seniority, and promotion. Such remedies were meant to correct a finding of discrimination by placing specific victims in the position they would have been in were it not for the discriminatory action of the defendant. And where a policy of discrimination deterred members of an underrepresented minority from even applying for opportunities, relief was to be granted if specific individuals could show that they would have applied but for their knowledge of the operation of the discriminatory policy.[17]

Bakke and *Fullilove* were the first major cases involving relief provided to individuals who were not the direct victims of specifiable acts of discrimination by the granting institution. Both cases have been controversial because in neither case was the relief provided for specific acts of discrimination officially attributed to the granting agency.

Regents of the University of California v. Bakke (1978)

The medical school at the University of California, Davis, opened in 1968 and the faculty devised a special program to insure the representation of minority students. This program reserved sixteen (out a total of one hundred slots for disadvantaged and minority students who were then evaluated in a separate admissions system. Alan Bakke was a White male who had been denied admission to the UC-Davis Medical School for two consecutive years. After his second refusal, he brought suit claiming his rights had been violated under the Fourteenth Amendment, the California constitution, and Title VI of the 1964 Civil Rights Act. In a split decision, five justices agreed, but they differed over whether it was unlawful for the school to take race into account in its admission process. Four justices argued that the university's decision violated Title VI, and Justice Powell argued further that it violated the Fourteenth Amendment, which he interpreted to proscribe not only invidious (meant to exclude) but benign (meant to include) racial classifications as well. Benign racial classifications were allowable, but only after a finding of discrimination by a judicial, legislative, or administrative body. "After such findings have been made, the governmental interest in preferring members of the injured groups at the expense of others is substantial, since the legal rights of the victims must be vindicated."[18] Justice Powell held that the university was not a body capable of making a finding of discrimination, and its goals could have been achieved by means other than classification based on the suspect category of race. Justices Brennan, White, Marshall, and

Blackmun dissented on this issue, arguing that the intent of the Fourteenth Amendment was to protect the class of former slaves and did not prohibit the use of racial classifications to remedy past discrimination. Benign uses of racial classifications should be held to an intermediate level of scrutiny such that they need not be necessary for (but only rationally related to) achieving an important governmental interest. Justice Brennan wrote:

> Congress can and has outlawed actions which have a disproportionately adverse and unjustified impact upon racial minorities and has required or authorized race-conscious action to put individuals disadvantaged by such impact in the position they otherwise might have enjoyed. Such relief does not require as a predicate proof that recipients of preferential advancement have been individually discriminated against; it is enough that each recipient is within a general class of persons likely to have been the victims of discrimination.[19]

Moreover, argued Justice Marshall, because of the complicity of the government in discrimination against Blacks, it had a compelling interest in initiating and supporting programs designed to bring Blacks into the mainstream of American life.[20] Also dissenting, Judge Blackmun maintained that it was proper for the university to make a finding of discrimination and that the remedial function of affirmative action was not possible without race-conscious measures: "In order to get beyond racism, we must first take account of race. There is no other way. And in order to treat some persons equally, we must treat them differently. We cannot—we dare not—let the Equal Protection Clause perpetrate racial supremacy."[21]

The Court was split on the many issues involved, and only Justice Powell argued that all racial classifications were legally subject to a strict rather than intermediate level of scrutiny. Nonetheless, Powell argued that race could be considered necessary in promoting the goal of diversity in the student body (although he did not insist that diversity be established as a compelling interest of the university). Despite many differences between the justices, the Court has remained consistent in allowing preferential treatment as a remedy for official findings of past discrimination. While Powell defended the view that such remedies should be limited to individuals, Brennan, Marshall, Blackmun, and White argued that remedies should be able to target groups as a whole.[22]

Fullilove v. Klutznick (1980)

The Public Works Employment Act of 1977 established a 10 percent set-aside of $4 billion in public-works funding for minority business enterprises (MBE). In the *Fullilove v. Klutznick* challenge to this set-aside, the Supreme Court acknowledged the right of Congress to use racial classifications in remedying past discrimination and held that an an adverse affect on a nonminority business amounted to a "sharing of the burden" by innocent parties. The Court denied that the set-aside was unduly *underinclusive* (failing to provide remedies to individuals who had been harmed by past discrimination) or *overinclusive* (providing benefits to members of the group who had not been harmed by past discriminatory action), and hence affirmed that it was narrowly tailored to meet the goal of ameliorating the present effects of past discrimination in government procurement programs. Moreover, the measure was temporary, ending with the final disbursement of funds allocated under the Public Works Act. Justice Stevens dissented, arguing that the MBE provision was overinclusive—providing benefits to members of the minority class who had not been harmed by past discriminatory action—and hence not narrowly tailored.

While early cases fit the classical model of compensation to specific individuals, *Bakke* and *Fullilove* directly addressed the issue of compensation to groups rather than individuals. In *Fullilove*, Powell, in a switch of positions, allowed that a remedy need not be directed to individuals who were the victims of specific instances of discrimination, but that Congress had the power to effect broad redistributive remedies. However, Justices Stewart, Rehnquist, and Stevens argued that remedies should be limited to specific individuals.

United Steelworkers v. Weber (1979)

In 1978, a union (the United Steelworkers of America) and a corporation (Kaiser Aluminum and Chemical Corporation) tacitly acknowledging that each had engaged in years of racial discrimination against Black workers, entered into a "voluntary" agreement to correct the discrepancy between the percentage of Blacks in skilled craft positions (0 percent) and the percentage of Blacks in the local labor force (39 percent) by reserving 50 percent of the openings in a training program sponsored by the corporation until the discrepancy was eliminated. Workers in skilled positions were paid substantially higher wages and, traditionally, admittance to such training programs was based on union membership and seniority. However, in accordance with the agreement, several Black workers were admitted over Brian Weber and other White workers with greater seniority. Weber brought suit, claiming that his rights (and those of others similarly situated) under Title VII were being violated.

Section 703j of Title VII stated that employers and unions could not be required to correct racial imbalances without a finding of discrimination, but Title VII encouraged voluntary agreements to correct such imbalances.[23] Without an official finding of past discrimination, specific percentages in hirings and promotions could not be viewed as remedial. Nonetheless, it was argued that the imbalance in the proportion of Blacks in skilled positions relative to their proportion in the local workforce was sufficient indication of past discrimination, and that Title VII was intended to redress such by redistributing resources and opportunities from Whites as a group to Blacks as a group. This was made clear in the Kaiser brief, which interpreted the intent of Title VII to be

> not only to compensate or make whole individuals, but also to achieve equality of employment opportunities and remove barriers that have operated in the past to favor . . . White employees over other employees. . . . This "prophylactic" objective . . . reaches beyond the person to the class. Compensation of an individual for harm he suffered does not assure persons of his race equal access to employment opportunities. Disadvantages to the group linger long after the injury to the individual has been enjoined and paid for.

Continuing with this point, the brief contended that "overcoming conditions that operate to the disadvantage of an identifiable group or class frequently requires the presence of that group in the workforce in significant numbers. Until that situation exists others may be deterred from applying or even seriously considering the possibility of doing so."[24]

On the other hand, the brief for Weber contended that the intent of the 50 percent quota was not to redress identifiable instances of discrimination against identifiable individuals, for none of those chosen for the training program were chosen because they were victims of past discrimination by the employer and union. Rather, the intent of the quota was to achieve a racially balanced workforce, and this was being done by discriminating against Whites, who had become the new victims of governmental policies to redistribute advancement opportunities to Blacks, irrespective of merit or seniority. Weber's brief argued that such policies would lead to greater (rather than less) racial animosity by fostering White resentment and Black stereotyping.

In deciding for the defendant (United Steelworkers), the Court held that the purpose of Title VII was to bring Blacks into the mainstream by opening employment opportunities in areas traditionally closed to them because of societal discrimination, and that this purpose could legitimately require using race-conscious policies. If Congress had wished to exclude such means, it could easily have worded 703j to read that Title VII would not "require or permit" preferential treatment, instead of merely stating that Title VII did not "require" preferential treatment. Justice Brennan concluded that the Kaiser-Steelworkers plan

> does not unnecessarily trammel the interests of White employees. The plan does not require the discharge of White workers and their replacement with new Black hires . . . Nor does the plan create an absolute bar to the advancement of White employees . . . Moreover, the plan is a temporary measure; it is not intended to maintain a racial balance, but simply to eliminate a manifest racial imbalance . . .[25]

Title VII should not be interpreted in such a way as to justify perpetuating the effects of prior discrimination, concurred Justice Blackmum. In dissent, Judge Rehnquist denied that it was the intent of Congress to interpret racial imbalance as sufficient to indicate discrimination and thereby justify compensatory measures.

Exploiting the sentiments expressed in the brief for Weber, Ronald Reagan made opposition to affirmative action a central part of his presidential campaign. Upon taking office in 1981, he proceeded to appoint executives (William Bradford Reynolds, Justice Department; Clarence Pendelton, Jr. and Clarence Thomas, Equal Employment Opportunities Commission) and Supreme Court justices (Antonin Scalia, Anthony Kennedy) who were hostile to the direction that affirmative action had taken. The budgets and staff of the EEOC and the Office of Federal Contract Compliance were cut, curtailing their ability to pursue cases of overt discrimination and affirmative action compliance.[26]

Firefighters Local Union No. 1784 v. Stotts (1984)

In 1980, the city of Memphis entered into a consent decree to remedy the exclusion of Blacks from employment and promotions, and to adopt long-range plans to increase the representation of minorities in the fire department. However, budgetary problems in 1981 required a reduction in government personnel and the city developed a plan in which some Whites would be laid off who had more seniority than some Blacks who were to be retained. The city argued that this was necessary in order to satisfy the consent decree to raise minority representation in the face of necessary layoffs and to avoid perpetuating the effects of past discriminatory actions. Because the action was voluntary, as in *Weber*, the city argued that it was unnecessary to limit its action to specific identifiable victims of past discrimination.

A majority of the Court ruled against the city, arguing that the consent decree originally entered into by the city did not include nullification of the seniority system in place, but rather only dealt with hiring and promotions. Title VII required retroactive seniority only to the specific victims of an official finding of discrimination. On the other hand, the Court's dissenting minority argued that Title VII should be interpreted, not in terms of the classical compensatory model aimed at providing relief to specific individuals, but in terms of the intent to redistribute opportunities to ensure that the effects of discrimination on Whites and Blacks are not perpetuated into the future.

Wygant v. Jackson Board of Education (1986)

In 1972, the Jackson County Board of Education of Jackson, Michigan entered into an agreement with the teachers' union that if layoffs were required, the percentage of minority teachers laid off would not exceed the percentage of minority teachers currently employed. Although there was no finding that the board had engaged in past discriminatory actions, the agreement was validated in state courts on the grounds that it addressed discrimination that was systemic rather than limited to a specific case. As a result, some White teachers were laid off who had more seniority than some of the Black teachers who were retained. The White teachers affected filed suit claiming that the action violated their rights

under the Fourteenth Amendment and Title VII. The action was upheld
by the district court and the Sixth Circuit Court of Appeals, on the
grounds that the action attempted to remedy societal discrimination
by providing important minority role models for both minority and
majority children.

The petitioners argued instead that "students had no constitutional
right to attend a school with a staff of any particular racial composi-
tion . . ."[27] As in *Firefighters Local Union No. 1784 v. Stotts*, the Reagan
administration supported the petitioners, arguing that (1) race-based
action must be strictly scrutinized and was justified only when applied to
remedy identified acts of past discrimination against specific individuals;
(2) no evidence was presented that the percentage of minority teachers in
the workforce exceeded the percentage employed by the school system;
and (3) the action required that innocent White employees be harmed
through discharge.[28]

In turn, respondents argued that state and local governments had a
compelling interest in eliminating the vestiges of past discrimination by
devising layoff plans that retained underrepresented minorities. Congress
had determined that discrimination in the public sector was more pervasive than in the private sector, and that governments had an obligation to
represent all of the people. Moreover, to require a finding of specific acts
of discrimination would inhibit voluntary compliance with the intent of
Title VII because an official finding of discrimination would expose the
offending agency to suits for back pay and other retroactive benefits,
whereas voluntary compliance avoided such extra expenses.[29] The plan
did not trammel the interests of White employees, since White and Black
employees shared the burden of layoffs, and, as in *Weber*, the plan was
temporary rather than permanent.

Again, the Court was split, with Justices Powell, Burger, Rehnquist,
O'Connor, and White voting to reject the layoff plan. Judge Powell held
that societal discrimination was too amorphous to justify the use of
remedies based on racial classifications, even when those classifications
were benign. Justice O'Connor agreed, but held that a finding of specific
discrimination was not necessary to satisfy strict scrutiny because that
would impede voluntary compliance.[30] Instead, she argued that the school
board had erred in basing its claim on the percentage of minority students
rather than on the percentage of minorities in the relevant labor market.

Judge Marshall, in dissent, held that achieving diversity would benefit all students, and that this was a sufficiently compelling interest of the state.[31] He rejected the contention that race-conscious layoff plans forced Whites to bear an unreasonable burden since in a layoff all (Black or White) who lose their jobs bear a burden. Rather, he insisted, the question was whether layoff plans must necessarily follow the pattern of seniority. He argued that the procedure was fair and narrowly tailored relative to other means of effecting a layoff (e.g., layoff by lottery). In all, though the layoff plan was rejected, a majority of the Court nonetheless expressed support for the view that specific findings of discrimination were not necessary to justify the use of race-based remedies.

Local 28, Sheet Metal Workers' Intern. Assn. v. EEOC (1986)

This landmark case centered on the Sheet Metal Workers Union, which was founded in 1888 for the purpose of forming all-White local affiliates. Local 28 was established in 1913, and membership was restricted to those who had completed its apprenticeship program. Applicants to the apprenticeship program in turn had to be recommended by a current union member, an arrangement that effectively excluded Blacks and other minorities. In 1964, the state initiated a suit that led a state court to order the use of a race-neutral testing procedure for selecting apprentices. When nine of the top ten scorers were Black, the union refused to admit them, suggesting instead that they must have cheated.[32]

As a result of a federal suit, Local 28 was found by the district court to be in violation of Title VII in recruitment, selection, training and admission to the union. Because of numerous "bad faith" attempts to evade and delay the admission of non-Whites, the union was ordered to cease discriminating and to admit 29 percent minorities (the percentage of non-Whites in the relevant labor pool in New York City) by July 1981. The union was found in contempt of court in 1982 and 1983, and was again ordered to admit 29 percent of new members from minority groups. The union appealed to the Supreme Court, arguing that the numerical goal amounted to a quota, that it rewarded individuals who had not been the specific victims of past discrimination by the union, and that the percentage of minority admits required by the lower courts exceeded the percentage of minorities available in the local labor market. The EEOC, under the Reagan administration (directed by Clarence Thomas), supported the union's brief.

Respondents argued that race-conscious remedies were not prohibited by Title VII and that the intent of Title VII was to effect broad-based redistribution of employment opportunities to Blacks. Prior rejection was not a necessary condition of an individual's receiving a remedy, for discrimination had been directed at Blacks as a group and not at specific individuals who merely happened to be Black. Rather, goals were meant to integrate Blacks into the workforce in the proportion that would have been had discrimination not occurred. "The impact on the favored class member is the same whether the proven victims receive their rightful place or whether the same number of persons (potential though not proven victims) occupy their places."[33]

The Supreme Court upheld the hiring goal and rejected the contention that Title VII limited relief to the actual victims of discrimination. Race-conscious relief furthered the intent of making employment opportunities available that had formerly been closed to minorities and reserved for Whites. Moreover, a union or employer's history of egregious discriminatory practices might continue to discourage minority applicants even after the agent had ceased to discriminate. In such cases, numerical goals might be the only form of remedy that would be effective in making opportunities broadly available. Title VII was not intended to limit relief to specific cases. For the majority, Justice Brennan stated: "The purpose of affirmative action is not to make identified victims whole but rather to dismantle prior patterns of employment discrimination and to prevent discrimination in the future."[34]

Because union membership was typically the result of sponsorship by existing union members, it was necessary that the union admit a substantial number of minority members to insure that its past discriminatory practices no longer served to discourage minority applications. Numerical goals were not a means to ensure a racial balance but were intended only as a "benchmark against which the court could gauge petitioners' efforts to remedy past discrimination."[35] And the goals were temporary. In dissent, Justices O'Connor and White argued that enforcing the goals during a time of recession amounted to a rigid quota that might operate to displace Whites with seniority. Justice Rehnquist and Chief Justice Burger opposed because they believed relief could only be granted to the specific individuals affected by specific past acts of discrimination.

Local 93, International Association of Firefighters v. City of Cleveland (1986)

In this important case involving non-victim-specific relief, the Supreme Court supported the city of Cleveland's voluntary agreement to reserve a certain number of promotions for minorities and establish goals for the future promotion of minorities, all within a fixed time period of less than nine years. One of the briefs for the respondents stated:

> In many situations, non-victim-specific relief is the only effective vehicle for achieving a work force which bears any reasonable resemblance to the work force which would have existed but for the employer's long standing discriminatory practices. . . . If unlawful discrimination were always detected and remedied immediately, then merely placing identified proven victims into their rightful place would produce a work force whose racial composition was not affected by discrimination . . . [but] direct victims cannot always be identified . . .[36]

And even when they could be identified, filing suit with the EEOC initiated a process that typically took three to six years to complete.

United States v. Paradise (1987)

United States v. Paradise was an especially flagrant case of discrimination by a governmental agency. Although Blacks made up 25 percent of the available labor force, no Black person had ever been hired as a state trooper in the state of Alabama. In 1972, a district court found that for four decades the Alabama Department of Public Safety had engaged in unlawful discrimination against minorities in violation of the Fourteenth Amendment, and ordered not only that they cease discriminating but that they also hire qualified Blacks in 50 percent of state trooper openings until Black employment approached the same level as in the local work-force (25 percent). The district court gave the following explanation of its order:

> The use of quota relief in employment discrimination cases is bottomed on the chancellor's duty to eradicate the continuing effects of past unlawful practices. By mandating the hiring of those who have been the object of discrimination, quota relief promptly operates to change the outward and

visible signs of yesterday's racial distinctions and thus, to provide an impetus
to the process of dismantling the barriers, psychological or otherwise, erected
by past practices.[37]

By 1978, no Blacks had been promoted to the rank of corporal or
above, and the Alabama Department of Public Safety entered into a
consent agreement to implement corrective procedures within a year.
However, no Blacks had been promoted by 1981, and a second agreement
was approved in which the promotional criteria would be reviewed to
determine if it had an adverse impact on Black candidates. In 1983,
the district court found the state troopers recalcitrance intolerable, the
promotions procedure was ruled to have a continuing adverse impact on
Blacks, and the Alabama Department of Public Safety was again ordered
to make at least 50 percent of state trooper promotions to corporal from
qualified Black candidates. The district court stressed that this promotions
quota was temporary and narrowly tailored to eliminate the present effects
of past discrimination, and could be terminated by the adoption of an
acceptable promotions procedure.

The Alabama Department of Public Safety, state trooper Phillip Paradise, Jr., and other Whites who would have been promoted by the
traditional criteria, and the U.S. government (under Reagan) sued for
relief from the lower court's ruling. They argued that the "quota" was
intended to achieve a racial balance rather than remedy past discrimination, that it placed an unnecessary burden on White troopers, and that it
thwarted their legitimate expectations.

In support of the lower court's order, the brief for the Southern Poverty
Law Center argued that a specific timetable and numerical target were
necessary if the goal of integrating the state troopers was to be achieved
in the foreseeable future, and that the 50 percent promotion requirement
was only to operate until the proportion of Blacks in the force approxi-
mated the proportion of Blacks in the relevant labor market. Justices
Brennan, Marshall, Blackmun, Powell, and Stevens upheld the promotions quota imposed by the lower court. They argued that the quota did
not unnecessarily burden White troopers because it was temporary, did
not require layoffs, and did not require the hiring of unqualified individuals. Moreover it was compensatory in that it provided relief to Black
troopers who had not been promoted. Justices O'Connor, Scalia, Rehnquist, and White dissented, arguing that the quota was meant to achieve
racial balance rather than remedy past discrimination.

Johnson v. Transportation Agency, Santa Clara County, California (1987)

This is one of the seminal cases involving affirmative action for women. In 1978, the Transportation Agency of Santa Clara, California voluntarily instituted an affirmative action plan for hiring and promoting women and minorities. Women and minorities were underrepresented in the agency relative to their availability in the relevant work pools, and were concentrated in the lower-paying jobs. The plan did not fix specific numerical goals but did allow that race and gender could be used in making hiring and promotions decisions.

Of two qualified candidates for promotion to a job staffed traditionally by men (radio dispatcher), an interview panel recommended the male applicant (Paul Johnson) while the county affirmative action office recommended the female applicant (Diane Joyce). The director chose Joyce and was then sued by the male applicant for violation of his rights under Title VII. According to Johnson, the transportation agency affirmative action plan barred the advancement of White males, was not temporary, and was not intended to remedy an established prior pattern of discrimination.

Standards established in *Weber* held that a valid affirmative action plan must operate to open traditionally segregated job categories, achieve (but not maintain) a racial balance, be temporary, and not bar the advancement of White (male) employees. The transportation agency argued that statistical disparities provided a sufficient evidentiary basis for prior discriminatory practice, which the plan was intended to remedy.[38] Nor did the plan unnecessarily bar the advancement of White employees. The court held that the agency plan met these standards. Concurring, Justice Stevens wrote:

> As construed in *Weber* . . . the statute does not absolutely prohibit preferential hiring in favor of minorities; it was merely intended to protect historically disadvantaged groups against discrimination and not to hamper managerial efforts to benefit members of disadvantaged groups that are consistent with that paramount purpose. The preference granted by respondent in this case does not violate the statute as so construed; the record amply supports the conclusion that the challenged employment decision served the legitimate purpose of creating diversity in a category of employment that has been almost an exclusionary province of males in the past. Respondent's voluntary decision is surely not prohibited by Title VII as construed in *Weber*.[39]

In dissent, Judge Scalia argued that the plan was not a remediation of past discrimination but the imposition of a goal of proportional representation by race and sex in the workplace. He suggested that women's past disinclination to pursue "unwomanly" jobs was as likely an explanation for the statistical disparity as was exclusion resulting from sexual discrimination.

Recent Rulings

An important shift in Supreme Court rulings occured in *Watson v. Fort Worth Bank and Trust* (1988) and *Wards Cove Packing Co. v. Antonio* (1989). In these cases, the Court reversed the *Griggs v. Duke Power Co.* (1973) ruling that the burden of proof rested with the employer to demonstrate the business necessity of employment practices that had a disparate impact on "protected minorities." Instead, the Court placed the burden of proof on the plaintiff to show that a specific employment practice caused discrimination against a "protected group."[40] The Civil Rights Bill of 1990 reversed the Supreme Court rulings in *Watson* and *Wards Cove*, and shifted the burden of proof back to the employer to show that an employment practice with a disparate impact on protected groups was job related and "consistent with business necessity." It also allowed women and minorities to collect damages up to $300,000 if it were proven that they were the victims of intentional discrimination.[41]

Croson and *Adarand* continued the trend of Supreme Court rulings placing greater restrictions on affirmative action measures. In *City of Richmond v. Croson* (1989), the Court held that state and local governments did not have the authority to use set-asides to remedy broad societal discrimination, as did the Congress in *Fullilove*. As of 1983, minority business enterprises (MBEs) received only 0.67 percent of the contracting funds spent by the city government of Richmond, Virginia, although the city was 50 percent Black. Acting to attenuate the effects of Richmond's long history of legally sanctioned segregation and preference for Whites, the city adopted the Minority Business Utilization Plan, which required at least 30 percent of the dollar value of construction contracts to go to MBEs.

Writing for the majority, Justice O'Connor argued that the city of Richmond had not demonstrated that the low percentage of awards to MBEs was the result of past racial discrimination. Rather, she cited nonracial factors such as "deficiencies in working capital, inability to meet bonding requirements, unfamiliarity with bidding procedures, and disability caused by an insufficient track record" as equally probable reasons accounting for the low participation rate. Nor, she continued, had the city eliminated the possibility that Black entrepreneurs simply preferred industries other than construction. All such factors could be addressed by means other than minority set-asides. Thus, minority set-asides had not been demonstrated to be necessary to eliminating the low participation rate.

The Court held that in order to pass the test of strict scrutiny, a direct causal link had to be established between a specific present injury and specific past or present acts of racial discrimination. O'Connor admitted that government had a compelling interest in preventing the use of government funds to support and perpetuate private discrimination. But, she held for the majority, there was no demonstration that lack of Black participation in city construction work was the specific effect of racial discrimination.[42]

In his dissent from the majority, Justice Marshall argued that the city had a compelling interest in intervening so as not to allow the effects of past discrimination to continue into the present and future, both in terms of the costs to the Black community and the benefits channeled to the White community. Lack of working capital and business experience were all traceable to legally sanctioned discrimination that denied Blacks these resources. The fact that there were so few minority construction firms was much more likely the result of reluctance to enter a field in which there was such pronounced racial hostility rather than the result of Blacks' antipathy to that kind of business.

In *Adarand Constructors, Inc. v. Pena* (1995) a contractor claimed that the federal government's practice of using race to identify "socially and economically disadvantaged individuals" for preferential treatment in the granting of highway construction contracts violated his constitutional rights of due process and equal protection. In deference to Congress's lawmaking powers, previous courts had applied only an intermediate level of scrutiny to federal policies involving racial classifications. However, in *Croson*, the Supreme Court required that state and local government policies using racial classifications be subject to strict scrutiny. In *Adarand*, the Court extended this requirement to the federal government.

The Court held that benign as well as invidious uses of racial classifications must satisfy the requirements of strict scrutiny, that is, be necessary for the achievement of a compelling government interest and be narrowly tailored to accomplish this end. This decision overturned the opinion in *Metro Broadcasting Inc. v. F.C.C.*, in which benign uses of racial classifications were required to meet only an intermediate level of scrutiny (i.e., be rationally related to accomplishing an important government end). Writing for the majority, Justice O'Connor applied the reasoning in *Croson* to federal initiatives:

> Absent searching judicial inquiry into the justification for such race-based measures, there is simply no way of determining what classifications are "benign" or "remedial" and what classifications are in fact motivated by illegitimate notions of racial inferiority or simple racial politics. Indeed, the purpose of strict scrutiny is to "smoke out" illegitimate uses of race by assuring that the legislative body is pursuing a goal important enough to warrant use of a highly suspect tool. The test also ensures that the means chosen "fit" this compelling goal so closely that there is little or no possibility that the motive for the classification was illegitimate racial prejudice or stereotype.[43]

In O'Connor's opinion, any local, state, or federal use of race to treat persons differently imposes an injury that must be necessary to achieve a compelling governmental interest. She held open the possibility, however, that there might in fact be policies using racial classifications that might be necessary to respond to the effects of racism (past and present): "we wish to dispel the notion that strict scrutiny is 'strict in theory, but fatal in fact'. . . . The unhappy persistence of both the practice and the lingering effects of racial discrimination against minority groups in this country is an unfortunate reality, and government is not disqualified from acting in response to it".[44]

Justice Scalia rejected even this possibility, however, arguing that "government can never have a 'compelling interest' in discriminating on the basis of race in order to make up for past racial discrimination." While individuals wronged by racial discrimination should be made whole, Scalia concluded that this does not apply to groups. "To pursue the concept of racial entitlement even for the most admirable and benign of purposes is to reinforce and preserve for future mischief the way of thinking that produced race slavery, race privilege and race hatred. In the eyes of government, we are just one race here. It is American."[45]

Justice Clarence Thomas advanced a similar view: "I believe that there is a moral and constitutional equivalence between laws designed to subjugate a race and those that distribute benefits on the basis of race in order to foster some current notion of equality."[46] Despite the good intentions of those who propose benign racial policies, Justice Thomas considered their use harmful because of the resentment they produce and the suspicions they feed that minorities are incapable of achieving without the "patronizing indulgence" of well-wishers.

Writing for the minority in dissent, Justice Stevens dismissed as ridiculous the suggestion that invidious and benign uses of racial classifications are indistinguishable. Such a view, he wrote, "would equate a law that made black citizens ineligible for military service with a program aimed at recruiting black soldiers."[47] He agreed that affirmative action programs may have some stigmatic costs to beneficiaries, but he pointed out that beneficiaries who felt such costs prohibitive could decline to be considered under affirmative action programs.

We see that one basic disagreement in the debate on affirmative action is the means by which a past of racist injuries is to be confronted. Critics of affirmative action argue that we should refuse to use racial classifications hereafter, in fear that such use may lead us to the very horrors we wish to leave behind. Defenders argue that we must use racial classifications in order to confront and undo the present effects of past and present manifestations of racism. In *Croson* and *Adarand*, the majority held that "the Fifth and Fourteenth Amendments to the Constitution protect persons, not groups." The following section will examine the claim implicit in this position, namely, that group disparities in the award of educational, employment, and entrepreneurial opportunities are to be allowed so long as specific victims cannot be identified.

Conceptual Issues

There are many interests that governments pursue—maximization of social production; equitable distribution of rights, opportunities, and services; social safety and cohesion; restitution—and those interests may conflict in various situations. In particular, governments as well as their constituents have a prima facie obligation to satisfy the liabilities they incur. One such liability derives from past and present unjust exclusionary acts depriving minorities and women of opportunities and amenities made available to other groups.

"*Backward looking*" arguments defend affirmative action as a matter of *corrective justice*, where paradigmatically the harmdoer is to make restitution to the harmed so as to put the harmed in the position the harmed most likely would have occupied had the harm not occurred. An important part of making restitution is the acknowledgment it provides that the actions causing injury were unjust and such actions will be curtailed and corrected. In this regard Bernard Boxill writes:

> Without the acknowledgement of error, the injurer implies that the injured has been treated in a manner that befits him. . . . In such a case, even if the unjust party repairs the damage he has caused . . . nothing can be demanded on legal or moral grounds, and the repairs made are gratuitous. . . . justice requires that we acknowledge that this treatment of others can be required of us; thus, where an unjust injury has occurred, the injurer reaffirms his belief in the other's equality by conceding that repair can be demanded of him, and the injured rejects the allegation of his inferiority . . . by demanding reparation.[48]

This view is based on the idea that restitution is a basic moral principle that creates obligations that are just as strong as the obligations to maximize wealth and distribute it fairly.[49] If x has deprived y of opportunities y had a right not to be deprived of in this manner, then x is obligated to return y to the position y would have occupied had x not intervened; x has this obligation irrespective of other obligations x may have. This can be illustrated another way as follows: Suppose y is deprived of t by x and we determine retroactively that y had a right to t. Then x has an obligation to return t to y or provide y with something else of equal value to t. In other words, x has an obligation to correct his or her effect on y, and restore y's losses.

A slightly different case illustrates a further point. Suppose x deprives y of the use of y's car for a day without y's consent and suppose further that x's use of the car produces $100 while y's use of the car would have produced only $50. In so far as an act is justified if it increases social utility, x is justified in having taken y's car. At most, x need only provide y with the value ($50) that y would have received if x had not taken the car. If y would not have used the car at all, presumably x would owe y only the depreciated value of the car resulting from its extra use. But though x increases social utility, x also deprives y of the exclusive use of y's private property. And to the extent that we consider the right of exclusive use important, it is wrong for x to profit from benefits that derive from x's enrichment through a violation of y's rights.

A further application of this principle involves the case where x is not a person but an entity, like a government or a business. If y was unjustly deprived of employment when firm F hired z instead of y because z was White and y Black, then y has a right to be made whole, that is, brought to the position he/she would have achieved had that deprivation not occurred. Typically, this involves giving y a position at least as good as the one he/she would have acquired originally and issuing back pay in the amount that y would have received had he/she been hired at the time of the initial attempt.

Most critics of preferential treatment acknowledge the applicability of principles of restitution to individuals in specific instances of discrimination. The strongest case is where y was as or more qualified than z in the initial competition, but the position was given to z because y was Black and z was White.[50] Subsequently, y may not be as qualified for an equivalent position as some new candidate z', but is given preference because of the past act of discrimination by F that deprived y of the position he or she otherwise would have received.

Some critics have suggested that, in such cases, z' is being treated unfairly. For z', as the most qualified applicant, has a right not to be excluded from the position in question purely on the basis of race; and y has a right to restitution for having unjustly been denied the position in the past. But the dilemma is one in appearance only. For having unjustly excluded y in the past, the current position that z' has applied for is not one that F is free to offer to the public. It is a position that is already owed to y, and is not available for open competition. Judith Jarvis Thompson makes a similar point:

> suppose two candidates [A and B] for a civil service job have equally good test scores, but there is only one job available. We could decide between them by coin-tossing. But in fact we do allow for declaring for A straightway, where A is a veteran, and B is not. It may be that B is a non-veteran through no fault of his own. . . . Yet the fact is that B is not a veteran and A is. On the assumption that the veteran has served his country, the country owes him something. And it is plain that giving him preference is not an unjust way in which part of that debt of gratitude can be paid.[51]

In a similar way, individual Blacks who have suffered from acts of unjust discrimination are owed something by the perpetrator(s) of such acts, and this debt takes precedence over the perpetrator's right to use his or her options to hire the most qualified person for the position in question.

Many White males have developed expectations about the likelihood of their being selected for educational, employment, and entrepreneurial opportunities that are realistic only because of the general exclusion of women and non-Whites as competitors for such positions. Individuals enjoying inflated odds of obtaining such opportunities because of racist and sexist practices are recipients of an "unjust enrichment."

Redistributing opportunities would clearly curtail benefits that many have come to expect. And given the frustration of their traditional expectations, it is understandable that they would feel resentment. But blocking traditional expectations is not unjust if those expectations conflict with the equally important moral duties of restitution and just distribution. It is a question, not of "is," but of "ought": not "Do those with decreased opportunities as a result of affirmative action feel resentment?" but "Should those with decreased opportunities as a result of affirmative action feel resentment?"

White males who are affected by such redistributions may be innocent in the sense that they have not practiced overt acts of racial discrimination, have developed reasonable expectations based on the status quo, and have exerted efforts that, given the status quo, would normally have resulted in their achieving certain rewards. Their life plans and interests are thus thwarted despite their having met all of the standards "normally" required for the achievement of their goals. Clearly, disappointment is not unnatural or irrational. Nonetheless, the resentment is not sufficiently justified if the competing moral claims of restitution and fair distribution have equal or even greater weight.

Since Title VII protects bona fide seniority plans, it forces the burden of rectification to be borne by Whites who are entering the labor force rather than Whites who are the direct beneficiaries of past discriminatory practices. Given this limitation placed on affirmative action remedies, the burden of social restitution may, in many cases, be borne by those who were not directly involved in past discriminatory practices. But it is generally not true that those burdened have not benefited at all from past discriminatory practices. For the latent effects of acts of invidious racial discrimination have plausibly bolstered and encouraged the efforts of Whites in roughly the same proportion as it inhibited and discouraged the efforts of Blacks. Such considerations are also applicable to cases where F discriminated against y in favor of z, but the make-whole remedy involves providing compensation to y′ rather than y. This suggests that y′ is an *undeserving beneficiary* of the preferential treatment meant to compensate for the unjust discrimination against y, just as z′ above appeared to be the innocent victim forced to bear the burden that z benefited from. Many critics have argued that this misappropriation of benefits and burdens demonstrates the unfairness of compensation to groups rather than individuals. But it is important that the context and rationale for such remedies be appreciated.

In cases of "egregious" racial discrimination, not only is it true that F discriminated against a particular Black person y, but F's discrimination advertised a general disposition to discriminate against any other Black person who might seek such positions. The specific effect of F's unjust discrimination was that y was refused a position he or she would otherwise have received. The latent (or dispositional) effect of F's unjust discrimination was that many Blacks who otherwise would have sought such positions were discouraged from doing so. Thus, even if the specific y actually discriminated against can no longer be compensated, F has an obligation to take affirmative action to communicate to Blacks as a group that such positions are indeed open to them. After being found in violation of laws prohibiting racial discrimination, many agencies have disclaimed further discrimination while in fact continuing to do so.[52] In such cases, the courts have required the discriminating agencies to actually hire and/or promote Blacks who may not be as qualified as some current White applicants until Blacks approach the proportion in F's labor force they in all likelihood would have achieved had F's unjust discriminatory acts not deterred them.

Of course, what this proportion would have been is a matter of speculation. It may have been less than the proportion of Blacks available in the relevant labor pool from which applicants are drawn if factors other than racial discrimination act to depress the merit of such applicants. This point is made again and again by critics. Some, such as Thomas Sowell, argue that cultural factors often mitigate against Blacks meriting representation in a particular labor force in proportion to their presence in the pool of candidates looking for jobs or seeking promotions.[53] Others, such as Michael Levin, argue that cognitive deficits limit Blacks from being hired and promoted at a rate proportionate to their presence in the relevant labor pool.[54] What such critics reject is the assumption that, were it not for pervasive discrimination and overexploitation, Blacks would be equally represented in the positions in question. What is scarcely considered is the possibility that, were it not for racist exclusions, Blacks might be over rather than under represented in competitive positions.

Establishing Blacks' presence at a level commensurate with their proportion in the relevant labor market need not be seen as an attempt to actualize some valid prediction. Rather, given the impossibility of determining what level of representation Blacks would have achieved were it not for racist discrimination, the assumption of proportional representation is the only *fair* assumption to make. This is not to argue that Blacks should be maintained in such positions, but their contrived exclusion merits an equally contrived rectification.[55]

Racist acts excluding Blacks affected particular individuals, but were directed at affecting the behavior of the group of all those similar to the victim. Likewise, the benefits of affirmative action policies should not be conceived as limited in their effects to the specific individuals receiving them. Rather, those benefits should be conceived as extending to all those identified with the recipient, sending the message that opportunities are indeed available to qualified Black candidates who would have been excluded in the past.

Reflecting the view of many critics of preferential treatment, Robert Fullinwider writes:

> Surely the most harmed by past employment discrimination are those Black men and women over fifty years of age who were denied an adequate education, kept out of the unions, legally excluded from many jobs, who have lived in poverty or close to it, and whose income-producing days are nearly at an end. Preferential hiring programs will have virtually no effect on these people at all. Thus, preferential hiring will tend not to benefit those most deserving of compensation.[56]

Because of the failure to appreciate the latent effects of discriminatory acts, this conclusion is flawed in two important respects. First, it limits the effect of specific acts of discrimination to the specific individuals involved. But the effect on the individual that is the specific object of a racist exclusion is not the only effect of that act, and may not be the effect that is most injurious or long term. For an invidious act affects not only y, but also y's family and friends. And it may well be that the greatest injury is, not to y, but to those who are deprived of sharing not only the specific benefits denied y, but also the motivation to seek (as y did) educational and employment opportunities they believe they would be excluded from (as y was).

Second, the conclusion that "preferential hiring will tend not to benefit those most deserving of compensation" fails to appreciate the extent that helping one member of a group may contribute indirectly to helping other members of that group. Clearly, admitting y' to medical school to compensate for not having admitted y in the past may nonetheless benefit y by increasing y's chance of obtaining medical services that otherwise might not be available.

We should conceive of the purpose of preferential treatment as being to benefit, not only the specific individuals directly affected by past racist acts, but also those counterfactually indicated in such acts. Affirmative action communicates not only to the specific Blacks and Whites involved in a particular episode, but to all Blacks and Whites that invidious racial discrimination is no longer the order of the day. Unless this is recognized, the purpose of preferential treatment will not be understood.

A similar criticism of the argument that preferential policies are a form of group restitution is based on the view that those in the group who have been harmed most by racial discrimination should receive the greatest compensation and those harmed least should receive the least compensation. But, it is argued, preferential treatment targets those with highest qualifications in the group and provides them with greater opportunities, while those without minimal qualifications are ignored.

One example of this kind of argument against preferential treatment is illustrated in Justice Stevens' dissent in the premier case concerning set-asides for minority businesses. The minority business enterprise provision of the Public Works Employment Act of 1977 mandated that at least 10 percent of the funds expended in the implementation of that bill be reserved for minority businesses. In upholding that provision in *Fullilove v. Klutznick*, the majority of the Supreme Court agreed that Congress, having established that the federal government had discriminated against minority businesses in the past, had the authority to attempt to rectify this by race-conscious measures intended to correct for past injuries and stop such injuries from being perpetuated into the future.

Justice Stevens dissented from the majority in this case, arguing that set-asides were both overinclusive and underinclusive in that they, as Ellen Frankel Paul puts it, "benefit most those least disadvantaged in the class, and leave the most disadvantaged, and, hence the most likely to be still suffering from the effects of past wrongs, with no benefits."[57] In a similar fashion, Alan Goldman argues: "Since hiring within the preferred group still depends upon relative qualifications and hence upon past opportunities for acquiring qualifications, there is in fact an inverse ratio established between past discrimination and present benefits, so that those who benefit most from the program, those who actually obtain jobs, are those who deserve to least."[58]

The major flaw I find in such arguments is the misconception that those with least qualifications are necessarily those who have been harmed most by racial discrimination. Prior to the initiation of affirmative action, we find that the Black/White earning ratio was progressively lower the more Blacks invested in themselves. That is, the more education a Black person had, the lower his or her earnings were relative to the earnings of a White person with a similar level of education. Thus, in 1949 (for men with 1 to 10 years experience) a Black college graduate (on the average) made 68 percent what a comparably educated White man made, while a Black high school graduate made 82 percent of what a White high school graduate made. In 1959 a Black college graduate (on the average) made 69 percent of the income of the average White college graduate while the Black high school graduate now made only 73 percent of the income of the White high school graduate.[59] And, in 1959 the average Black man with a college degree was earning less than the average White man with only eight years of formal education.[60]

These figures indicate how, prior to affirmative action, racial discrimination operated to disadvantage Blacks with higher levels of education progressively more than it disadvantaged those with less education.[61] That Blacks of equal achievement and productivity benefited less than Whites of similar qualifications is a well known feature of slavery and segregation. It is less appreciated that (on the average) benefits decreased with increases in ability, potential, and qualifications relative to similarly situated Whites. Providing equal opportunity thus means more than simply moving Black people above the poverty line, for this would do nothing for those whose ability would likely have placed them far above the poverty line, were it not for the increasing hostility at higher levels of achievement. While it might appear that Black businessmen have been harmed least by racial discrimination, the fact is that many such individuals may in fact have been harmed most, relative to what they could have achieved if racial discrimination had not impeded their efforts.[62]

Of course, there are many among the least well off who have the potential to have done much better than they have in fact done. This is true for both Blacks and Whites. Affirmative action attempts to target those whose potential has been depressed as a result of racial discrimination, and provide them with opportunities they would not have otherwise.[63] While many Blacks among the least well off would have done better but for racial discrimination, it is equally plausible that many Blacks among the most well off would have done better but for racial discrimination. It follows that equalizing opportunity and erasing the effects of racial discrimination, past and present, should target both the overrepresentation of Blacks among the poor and the underrepresentation of Blacks among the well off.

These considerations are not meant to deny that there may be many reasons why a particular individual may have been denied opportunities other than because of racial discrimination. To illustrate, suppose y goes for a job interview and x, the interviewer, doesn't like brown-eyed people, and y happens to be brown eyed. Interviewer x gives y a low rating and y doesn't get the job, though by "objective" criteria, y was qualified. Can y bring suit against x for unjust discrimination? The answer is no. The Civil Rights Acts of 1964, 1972, and 1991 prohibit discrimination on the basis of race, sex, national origin, and religion. There is no prohibition against discrimination on the basis of education, level of skill, or eye color. Education and skill level are used to discriminate between prospective employees, because they are taken to be good indicators of whether the applicant will be able to perform at or above the level required. But eye color does not appear relevant in predicting a person's future performance (though there might be some cases in which eye color was relevant, for example, as a model for a particular brand of cosmetics), and so our moral intuition is that using this factor in deciding between candidates is a form of unjust discrimination. There is, however, no legal prohibition against discrimination on the basis of eye color.

There are many factors that influence individual prospective employers in choosing between candidates—the way they dress, their posture and demeanor, their choice of cologne, hairstyle, personal relationship to the employer—and many if not most may be totally irrelevant to the person's ability to perform the job in question. But it is not always immoral to choose a candidate based on factors irrelevant to their ability to perform, as in the case of hiring a person because he or she is a close relative. In any case, it would be impossible to identify all such factors and legislate against them.

Civil rights legislation prohibits using factors that historically have been used systematically to exclude certain groups of individuals from opportunities generally available to members of other groups. Thus, the disabled have systematically been excluded relative to the physically normal, women excluded relative to men, Blacks excluded relative to Whites, Muslims and Jews excluded relative to Christians, and so on.

We can expect many individuals equal with respect to their productive capacity to have been treated unequally by the market because of random factors that influence the choices of decision makers for available opportunities. Within both excluded and preferred groups, there will be some who are better off than others, based on random factors that have influenced their economic destiny. But it is only at the level of the group that systematic as opposed to random factors can be distinguished. Economist Lester Thurow estimates that "70 to 80 percent of the variance in individual earnings is caused by factors that are not within the control of even perfect governmental economic policies," and he concludes: "The economy will treat different individuals unequally no matter what we do. Only groups can be treated equally."[64]

Because of a history of racist exclusion from educational, employment, and investment opportunities, Blacks generally have a lower ratio of relevant job-related skills and attitudes than Whites. Eliminating racism would do nothing to eliminate this deficit in human capital, which in itself is sufficient to ground a continuing prejudice against Blacks.

As Owen Fiss has argued, preferential treatment for a disadvantaged group provides members of that group with positions of power, prestige, and influence that they would otherwise not attain in the near future.[65] Such positions empower both the individuals awarded those positions as well as the group they identify with and are identified with by others. Individuals awarded such positions serve as models that others within their group may aspire to, and (more often than not) provide the group with a source of defense and advocacy that improves the status of the group.

Fiss acknowledges, as many critics have stressed, that preferential treatment might encourage claims that Blacks do not have the ability to make it on their own, thereby perpetuating the myth of Black inferiority.[66] But I do not see this as a serious problem. For the assumption of Black inferiority is used to explain both why Blacks do not occupy prestigious positions when they are in fact absent from such positions and why they do occupy them when they are in fact present in such positions. The assumption of Black inferiority exists with either option, and Blacks who do occupy positions they would likely not occupy but for affirmative action are not losing credibility they otherwise might have. On the other hand, Blacks who do occupy such positions and perform at or above expectation do gain a credibility they otherwise would not have.[67]

An enduring legacy of racism (and sexism) is the presumption that Blacks (and women) are generally less competent and undeserving of nonmenial opportunities. Thus, the issue is not whether Blacks will be considered incompetent, but whether the effects of that assumption will continue. "The ethical issue is whether the position of perpetual subordination is going to be brought to an end for our disadvantaged groups, and if so, at what speed and at what cost."[68]

In a recent article, Ellen Frankel Paul presents an argument that has been repeated with many variations by critics of claims that restitution is owed Blacks for the ravages of slavery and discrimination.[69] How, the argument goes, could Black Americans be restored to the position they would have occupied but for slavery, since if it were not for slavery, they would be living under even worse conditions.

> If not for the slave trade, most of the descendants of the slaves would now be living in Africa under regimes known neither for their respect for human rights, indeed for human life, nor for the economic well-being of their citizens. The typical denizen of one of these states, I dare speculate, would envy the condition of the Black teenage mother on welfare in one of this country's worst inner cities. . . . if we take the restorative element of compensatory justice literally, Blacks in America would be owed worse lives than the ones that they currently live: a not terribly satisfactory conclusion.[70]

Michael Levin makes a similar argument:

> "Take Mr. X, an American Black, who we think is worse off than he would have been had his African ancestors not conquered a neighboring tribe that was then raided by slave traders; had his ancestors respected territorial boundaries, Mr. X might now be a sickly native of Uganda."[71]

Such arguments are as demeaning as they are disingenuous. First, had the African slave trade to the Americas not existed, there would be no descendants of such slaves. It is likely that those individuals who in fact were enslaved would have had children had they not been enslaved, but it is highly improbable that any of those children would be identical to the particular individuals conceived under slavery. In all probability, a particular woman captured in Africa and enslaved in America would, had she remained in Africa, have had children by someone altogether different from the person(s) she had children by under slavery.

Thus, it makes no sense at all to speak as if the descendants of slaves would be in a better or worse condition had there been no slavery, since the descendants of slavery would not exist had there been no slavery. Moreover, it makes no sense to speak as if Africa would have been as badly off as it now is had there been no slave trade and colonization. Given any benefit of the doubt as to the ability of Africans to develop modern cultures, Africa would probably be much better off than it currently is.[72]

Similar considerations hold for the case of African Americans. While it is true that the class of African Americans as now constituted would not exist were it not for the slave trade, it does not follow that there would be no African Americans had there been no slave trade. For it is likely that Africans would have come to the United States in the same manner that other ethnic groups came to America, voluntarily to seek their good fortune. And presumably, had Africans come to the Americas in that way, they would not have been subject to the stigma, contempt, and discrimination deriving from the racist justifications of slavery. Had Africans come to the Americas voluntarily, African Americans as a group would exist, though the group would be constituted by a completely different set of individuals. Such individuals would have been able to pass on their skills and accumulated wealth to their progeny, who would most likely be unburdened by a recent past of legally sanctioned racist exclusions.

African Americans cannot demand compensation for having been brought into existence as a result of the slave trade, on the grounds that they would have been better off had they been brought into existence through ancestors who came to America voluntarily. But they can demand compensation for the exploitation they have endured under slavery and segregation.[73] Even Paul is willing to admit this:

Upon Emancipation, certainly the [freed] slaves should have received compensation along the lines of that given by the Federal Republic of Germany to the victims of the Nazis. That this was not done . . . is an omission that compounds the historical injustice committed against those enslaved. Under a theory of compensatory justice to groups of actual victims of heinous state acts, slavery as practiced in the South is archetypically the kind of rights violation that requires recompense . . .[74]

Given that this was not done she concludes that the classical model of compensatory justice provides only "vicarious and indirect recompense" for the injuries passed on to the progeny of the slaves, plus the guarantee "that they shall live henceforth under a government that no longer perpetrates such acts."[75]

However, I believe that government perpetrates the injuries of slavery and segregation if it initiates no effort to correct for those injuries.[76] Refusing to act when action is called for can be as great a source of injury as inappropiate intervention. It does no good to cite a statute of limitations, since demands for restitution have been made continuously since slavery was abolished. The Freedmen's Bureau was initially conceived as a means of providing freed slaves with the education and capital necessary to make them at least self-sufficient. But these amenities were withdrawn in favor of a system that perpetuated the subordination of freed slaves through political exclusion, inadequate educational facilities, job reservations, and housing segregation.[77]

Paul also repeats the argument that if we take compensatory justice to apply to groups rather than to specific individuals, we are left with the further unsatisfactory results that preferential treatment and set-asides tend to compensate those who were least harmed by the unjust discrimination of governments in the past and ignores those who were most harmed. I have challenged this view earlier. But even if we were to grant that Blacks whose potential has been developed to the point of manifesting at least minimal qualifications have been harmed less by racism than Blacks whose potential has not been so developed, it does not follow that more-qualified Blacks have not been harmed and thus are not due any appropriate degree of compensation.[78] Moreover, helping those in the group with qualifications is an important way of helping those who are least well off. Despite the exodus of Black professionals from the inner cities, Black doctors, lawyers, and businesses continue to serve other Blacks to a higher degree than professionals of other races. Ignoring such considerations allows Paul and fellow critics to dismiss the validity of providing restitution to groups, and insist instead on the classical model limiting restitution to individuals.

The unjust appropriation of wealth from Blacks did not end with the abolishment of slavery. White immigrants benefited substantially from racism by being given preference for benefits over Blacks. The free White artisan and working class were especially hostile to Blacks because they viewed freed slaves as potential competitors. "They were strongly opposed to any lowering of the status of crafts by their association with slaves or freed Blacks. Instead, the most low paying semi-skilled activities were soon identified as 'nigger work', while the better paying skilled crafts were exclusively confined to White workers."[79] In the economic struggle that capitalism encourages, racism became a formidable weapon used by the White working class in order to eliminate competition from Black workers. As a result, the status of Blacks after the abolishment of slavery was (with the exception of the radical reconstruction era) simply a continuation of conditions that had prevailed during slavery.[80]

The rise of labor unions benefited White workers by giving them enhanced bargaining power with employers. But more often than not, unions did not admit Black members and typically insisted on a closed shop, which meant that any Black workers that may already have been working in a firm would be fired and replaced by White union workers. Typically, one became a union member by being recommended by someone who was already a member. It was the norm for the progeny of union members to themselves become union members. As such, it is not merely the progeny of slave holders that owe restitution. Rather, as Bernard Boxill has argued, the opportunities denied Blacks have been distributed throughout the White community at large, and it is that community as a whole that owes the Black community restitution.

In response to the claim that Blacks are owed restitution for the injuries suffered under slavery, segregation, and other racially exclusionary practices, some critics have objected that contemporary Whites should not be required to accept responsibility for something they had no choice in. Whatever benefits they may have received, they had no choice in receiving. And since a person or party can be held morally responsible only for something that they could have done or avoided doing, it is unjust to require restitution from those least responsible for the injuries inflicted by segregation and racism. As one critic puts it, "it is morally absurd to penalize [someone] for an evil that he could not have prevented."[81]

But the morally relevant issue is not whether the beneficiaries of unjust acts are responsible for the unjust acts, but whether the beneficiaries sincerely attempt to make restitution for their continuing enrichment from such acts. Certainly, contemporary Whites are not responsible for many of the current injuries suffered by Blacks. But they are responsible for continuing to profit from benefits that derive from such injuries. Continuing to benefit from acts of injustice creates a liability to make restitution for them, at least to the degree of relinquishing the undeserved benefits.

Another objection to preferential treatment as a form of restitution derives from the principle, central to corrective justice, that those most responsible for harm should bear the primary cost of restitution and those most harmed should receive the greatest share of the restitution. However, while older Whites are most likely to be responsible for the injuries of racism, it is young Whites seeking educational and employment positions who are forced to bear the primary cost of restitution. Likewise, while it is older Blacks with the least education and training who bear the greatest injuries from the legacy of slavery and segregation, it is young Blacks with the highest qualifications who are the beneficiaries of preferential treatment.

But again, there is little need to quibble with the fact that older White workers are the direct beneficiaries of past racist exclusions, and are now granted a strong measure of protection by seniority systems in recognition of their subsequent investment of time, energy, and effort in those positions. But young Whites are the indirect beneficiaries of past racist acts and the direct beneficiaries of current ones. Institutional racism gives young Whites a decided advantage over young Blacks because they have generally received better educational and entrepreneurial opportunities, and because they are less subject to stigmatized stereotypes.

Prior to affirmative action, Blacks were penalized in direct proportion to their level of qualification. Those with higher levels of qualifications were typically subjected to greater prejudice and higher rates of exclusion from opportunities to develop and profit from those qualifications. Among Blacks harmed most by racism would thus be individuals with maximum potential who were prevented by racist exclusions from developing that potential into even minimal qualifications.[82] However, the fact that preferential treatment does not reach Blacks who have been most harmed by racism is no criticism for helping those less harmed. One does not condemn aspirin as a remedy for headaches because it does not also remedy migraines.[83]

Reparations without Affirmative Action

Glenn Loury, in a recent collection of essays, points out that there will always be inequalities between groups, because there will always be a group that is worse off, namely, the group composed of those with least income and wealth.[84] It is only when we define groups in other than purely economic terms that group inequality can become a true social problem. Equal opportunity depends, not just on the potential of an individual, but on the opportunities of those with whom that individual is socially affiliated. As Loury puts it: "Whom you know affects what you come to know and what you can do with what you know."[85] It is through social networks that information flows about economic opportunities and how to effectively take advantage of such opportunities.

Because of this country's history of racial segmentation and discrimination, Blacks have been deprived of capital to a degree that, left to purely market mechanisms, would perpetuate itself indefinitely into the future. As such, Loury recommends that "government intervention aimed specifically at counteracting the effects of historical disadvantage, and taking as given existing patterns of affiliation, will be required."[86]

> preferentially greater expenditures (not merely equalization of spending) by public institutions that serve large numbers of poor Black people . . . should be permitted . . . because we cannot expect laissez-faire policies to produce equality of opportunity between social groups when these groups have experienced differential treatment in the past . . .[87]

While Loury does not advocate a color-blind policy, he also does not advocate a policy of preferential treatment for Blacks in employment, educational, and business opportunities. For Loury, affirmative action policies have focused on helping those Blacks who are most well off, at the expense of ignoring the needs of the Black poor. While he supports weak affirmative action policies of outreach and antidiscrimination, he opposes stronger versions of affirmative action involving preferential treatment. He asserts that quotas and set-asides have had a negligible trickle down effect on Blacks who are least well off, and has helped primarily Blacks with more education attain positions in the more prestigious occupations.[88]

This is a criticism made by many critics of affirmative action, which suggests that the recipients of affirmative action are college-educated, white-collar workers hired by firms to display their commitment to minorities. As a matter of fact, however, it has been in the skilled, blue-collar categories that affirmative action has had its primary impact, forcing labor unions and employers to admit minorities and women to jobs they had traditionally been excluded from.[89]

Most of the major cases that have come before the Supreme Court have involved blue-collar rather than white-collar jobs. Recall that the issue in question in *Griggs* was whether a high school diploma could be required for a certain category of jobs; in *Weber*, the issue involved training for a skilled craft position; in *Sheetmetal Workers*, it was admittance to a craft union; in *Paradise*, it involved positions as state troopers; in *Firefighters*, the positions in question required firefighting skills; in *Johnson v. Transportation Agency*, the position in question was that of a radio dispatcher.

The initiation of strong affirmative action during the early 1970s produced a period of extraordinary growth in the participation of Blacks throughout the labor force. Between 1960 and 1993, the proportion of Blacks employed among telephone operators went from 2.6 percent to 21.0 percent, among firefighters it went from 2.5 percent to 7.5 percent, among accountants and auditors it went from 1.6 percent to 7.0 percent, among secretaries it went from 2.0 percent to 7.7 percent, among retail salespersons it went from 2.4 percent to 9.7 percent, among electricians it went from 2.2 percent to 6.1 percent, while among lawyers it only went from 1.3 percent to 2.7 percent.[90] Between 1970 and 1993 Black employment increased from 23,796 to 70,095 among police officers, from 14,145 to 40,626 among electricians, from 10,633 to 30,774 among bank tellers, from 3,914 to 29,250 among health workers, from 2,501 to 11,407 among pharmacists, and from 2,227 to 8,080 among professional athletes.[91] Clearly, the major effects of affirmative action have not been in white collar and executive positions.

It is unlikely that such results would have been achieved if labor unions, large businesses, and government agencies had not felt under pressure to hire and promote qualified Black candidates. Many economists have argued that firms that refuse to hire qualified Black workers will have higher wage costs than firms that will hire qualified Blacks, and that competition between firms will tend to favor those with lower costs and higher productivity.[92] However, there are many conditions under which the benefits of utilizing racial stereotypes might outweigh the costs of missing competent employees in the group discriminated against and of hiring incompetent employees in the group discriminated for. Though a prospective employer might believe that a particular Black applicant might perform a certain job as well as a competing White applicant, it might hire the White worker to avoid losing business because of the biases of its customers. A firm might also find racial discrimination in favor of Whites beneficial if it diminished the prospect of costly shutdowns and enhanced satisfaction and cooperation among existing workers.

In a slack labor market, statistical discrimination against Blacks might have negligible costs and substantial benefits. But the profitability of such discrimination does not make it acceptable, anymore than slavery's profitability was sufficient for its moral justification.[93] We can expect the influence of cost-benefit factors in hiring and promotions to be attenuated only if society intervenes to make discriminating on the basis of race (gender and disability) more costly than not discriminating on such bases. For under appropriate conditions, it is not irrational to discriminate against Black applicants and in favor of White applicants.

Despite laws making it illegal, patterns of racial discrimination persist in both the public and private spheres. Discrimination in the hiring, promotion, and enforcement practices of law enforcement agencies is one indication of its pervasiveness in agencies of the government. Numerous suits and testimonials document continuing examples of discriminatory practices in federal, state, and local law enforcement agencies, among major retailers, financial institutions, and newspapers.[94]

In addition to documented cases, numerous research studies point to the persistence of discriminatory practices. Despite the prominence of Blacks in sports, studies have shown that Black athletes generally make less money than their White counterparts with similar skills, and that they are valued less as they achieve more prestigious positions. This is attributed to "consumer discrimination," where consumers consistently value Whites over equally qualified Blacks.[95] Likewise, in purchasing cars and other forms of real property, studies indicate that Blacks and women are charged substantially higher prices than similarly situated White men.[96]

Studies also document the continuing phenomena of "redlining," where lending institutions systematically discriminate against Blacks relative to similarly situated Whites. The term "redlining" derives from a practice initiated by the Federal Housing Authority in which certain sections on a map were outlined in red in order to indicate areas in which higher standards should be applied to applicants for mortgage loans. A study by the Boston area Federal Reserve Board in 1989 found that banks turned down Black loan applicants at a rate twice that of White loan applicants. A later study found that well-qualified Blacks and Whites were treated similarly, but marginally qualified Blacks and Hispanics were rejected at twice the rate of similarly qualified Whites.[97] This effectively made it twice as hard for a marginally qualified Black or Hispanic to acquire property as a similarly qualified White person.

In seeking employment, a study involving matched pair Black and White job applicants showed that in 476 hiring audits White applicants advanced further in 20 percent of the audits and received job offers in 15 percent more audits than similarly qualified Black applicants. Despite the alleged prevalence of "reverse discrimination" in hiring, Blacks advanced further in only 7 percent of the audits, and received job offers while their White counterparts did not in only 5 percent of the audits. This means that discrimination in favor of White applicants was three times more likely than discrimination in favor of Black applicants.[98]

Enforcement of antidiscrimination laws on a case-by-case basis has proven insufficient, as indicated by the fact that the EEOC currently has a backlog of over eighty thousand cases, with the average case taking some three to six years to adjudicate.[99] Because of the pervasive and amorphous character of racism and sexism, it is not possible to identify and prosecute all instances of such practices.[100] Discrimination in favor of non-Whites and women through preferential policies has evolved as a means to counter continuing discrimination against them. Preferential policies place members of historically oppressed groups in positions that discrimination makes it unlikely they would otherwise achieve, and empowers them to make decisions that reduce the past and present effects of racism and sexism. Without active intervention by government, there is little incentive for firms, unions, or customers to cease discriminating.[101]

Loury cites as a primary cost of preferential treatment the loss of respect from fellow colleagues for Blacks hired and promoted through preferential treatment. But lack of respect for Blacks is likely to remain or even increase if Blacks continue to be excluded from positions of public prestige and responsibility. Loury claims that preferential treatment may remove the incentive for Blacks to develop the skills necessary to compete success-fuly for available opportunities. He proposes this as a theoretical possibil-ity, one he insists he has no empirical justification for, but he proceeds to elaborate it into an impressive econometric model. However imposing, his argument altogether ignores the possibility that putting Blacks into positions they are otherwise unlikely to achieve might provide them with an incentive to develop skills that lead to even higher level opportunities.

It is not clear to me why viewing preferential treatment as an incentive for developing further qualifications is not as plausible as viewing it as a disincentive for developing such qualifications. Without basic qualifica-tions, opportunities are nil. With qualifications, but without affirmative action, opportunities are possible but not probable. With qualifications and affirmative action, opportunities become not only possible, but also more probable. Loury's position amounts to viewing Blacks as lacking pride and ambition, and as being satisfied with the lowest levels of achievement made possible by the redistributive effects of affirmative action. Thus, while I support Loury's call for a form of reparation, I find his criticism of preferential policies for the qualified unconvincing.

Strong affirmative action attempts to guarantee that Blacks do not continue to be disadvantaged because of their race. Some may object to the doubt that affirmative action may raise as to the extent their achieve-ments are based on personal merit. Certainly they have the option of refusing awards that take race (or sex) into account.[102] But there should be no doubt that Blacks suffer systemic disadvantages in the competition for educational, employment, and investment opportunities. Preferential policies are one means of offsetting this disadvantage.

The justification for preferential treatment as a form of restitution is often criticized because, to the extent that it is conceived of as a repayment for past deprivations, it seems to apply independent of the current status of the recipient. To return to the basic model, if x has wrongly deprived y of a benefit, x has an obligation to provide y with restitution whether y needs it or not. It may be that x accidentally knocked an ice cream cone from y's hands while x was on her way to buy minimum food needs for herself. On a model of strict restitution, x owes y another ice cream cone. However, most people would consider it inappropriate to insist that x replace y's indulgence at the expense of denying x a necessity. Even in the case where x unintentionally deprived y of a basic need, it is debatable whether x is obligated to replace it if doing so deprives x of an equal or greater need.[103]

In similar fashion, it appears morally improper to insist that the son of a wealthy Black family be given preferential treatment over the daughter of a poor White family. While there may be some cases in which this might be justified (e.g., in order to provide needed role models or services in a particular area for Blacks), generally speaking such an award would be improper.[104]

Our moral duties conflict, and so often do governmental interests. This means that, in some cases, the duty to provide restitution may be superseded by other duties. Defenders of preferential policies need not deny this. For y to insist that x sacrifice a basic need in order to provide y with a lost opportunity to enjoy a luxury is myopic and selfish. Likewise, to expect poor Whites to sacrifice opportunities to well-off Blacks as a matter of course ignores the fact that injuries of class may in many cases be as great or greater than injuries of race.[105]

Another argument against preferential treatment takes the position that even if x wrongly deprives y of the ability to do t, then it does no good to give y preferential treatment for a position requiring t, since y no longer has the ability to do t. As such, putting y in a position he or she cannot fulfill is both damaging to y and to society at large. But this is an argument that no advocate of preferential treatment need disagree with. In every case, restitution must be appropriate to the injury. In some cases, the appropriate restitution might be providing y the opportunity to develop skills he likely would have acquired were it not for the injury suffered because of x. On the other hand, if the injury has permanently disabled y from being able to do t, then putting y in a position requiring that he or she do t is unfair to all concerned. A person must be able to do t before he or she can be considered a viable candidate for a position requiring t.[106]

The concept of merit is one that has been extensively debated since the onset of preferential policies in affirmative action, and this debate has been productive not just for women and minorities, but for the majority as well. It has helped us recognize that academic achievement is only one indication of how well a person might be able to perform the tasks required in the practice of a profession. One of the key pieces of evidence in *Griggs v. Duke Power Co.* was that Whites hired without a high school diploma performed their jobs as effectively as Whites hired with a high school diploma. Although requiring a high school diploma would have excluded Blacks at a higher rate than Whites, that requirement would also have excluded many Whites who were otherwise competent for the positions in question.

Forward-Looking Justifications of Affirmative Action

While Loury defends a form of reparation for Blacks but rejects preferential treatment, others have defended preferential treatment but denied that it should be viewed as a form of reparation. This latter group rejects "backward looking" justifications of affirmative action and defends it instead on "forward-looking" grounds that include distributive justice, minimizing subordination, and maximizing social utility.

Thus, Ronald Fiscus argues that backward-looking arguments have distorted the proper justification for affirmative action policies.[107] Backward-looking arguments depend on the paradigm of traditional tort cases, where a specific individual x has deprived another individual y of a specific good t through an identifiable act a, and x is required to restore y to the position y would have had, had a not occurred. But typically, preferential treatment requires that x' (rather than x) restore y' (instead of y) with a good t' that y' supposedly would have achieved had y not been deprived of t by x. The displacement of perpetrator (x' for x) and victim (y' for y) gives rise to the problem of (1) White males who are innocent of acts having caused harm nonetheless being forced to provide restitution for such acts; and (2) Blacks who were not directly harmed by those acts nonetheless becoming the principal beneficiaries of restitution for those acts.

For many, the backward-looking justification for affirmative action makes it seem that innocent White males are forced to bear the principle burden for correcting the wrongs of the past, and that the least harmed Blacks are the undeserving beneficiaries of their unjust sacrifice. This is clearly the sense expressed in Justice Scalia's opposition to affirmative action:

> My father came to this country when he was a teenager. Not only had he never profited from the sweat of any Black man's brow, I don't think he had ever seen a Black man. There are, of course many White ethnic groups that came to this country in great numbers relatively late in its history—Italians, Jews, Poles—who not only took no part in, and derived no profit from, the major historic suppression of the currently acknowledged minority groups,

but were, in fact, themselves the object of discrimination by the dominant Anglo-Saxon majority. To be sure, in relatively recent years some or all of these groups have been the beneficiaries of discrimination against Blacks, or have themselves practiced discrimination, but to compare their racial debt . . . with that of those who plied the slave trade, and who maintained a formal caste system for many years thereafter, is to confuse a mountain with a molehill. Yet curiously enough, we find that in the system of restorative justice established by the Wisdoms and the Powells and the Whites, it is precisely these groups that do most of the restoring. It is they who, to a disproportionate degree, are the competitors with the urban Blacks and Hispanics for jobs, housing, education.[108]

Similarly Judge Richard Posner writes:

The members of the minority group who receive preferential treatment will often be those who have not been the victims of discrimination while the nonminority people excluded because of preferences are unlikely to have perpetrated, or to have in any demonstrable sense benefitted from, the discrimination."[109]

Fiscus argues that the backward-looking argument reinforces the perception that preferential treatment is unfair to innocent White males, and so long as this is the case, both the courts and the public are likely to oppose strong affirmative action policies such as quotas, set-asides, and other preferential treatment policies.

In contrast, Fiscus recommends that preferential treatment be justified in terms of distributive justice, which as a matter of equal protection, "requires that individuals be awarded the positions, advantages, or benefits they would have been awarded under fair conditions," that is, conditions under which racist exclusion would not have precluded Blacks from attaining "their deserved proportion of the society's important benefits." Conversely, "distributive justice also holds that individuals or groups may not claim positions, advantages, or benefits that they would not have been awarded under fair conditions."[110] These conditions jointly prohibit White males from claiming an unreasonable share of social benefits and protects White males from having to bear an unreasonable share of the redistributive burden.

Fiscus takes the position that any deviation between Blacks and Whites from strict proportionality in the distribution of current goods is evidence of racism. Thus, if Blacks were 20 percent of a particular population but held no positions in the police or fire departments, that is indicative of past and present racial discrimination. While discrimination exists with respect to many characteristics other than race (i.e., height and attractiveness), the Fourteenth Amendment prohibits such in the case of race.[111] As such, deviations in the distribution of goods with respect to groups defined by race are subject to legal review, unlike deviations in the distribution of goods with respect to groups defined by attractiveness.

Because the Equal Protection Clause of the Fourteenth Amendment protects citizens from statistical discrimination on the basis of race, the use of race as the principal reason for excluding certain citizens from benefits made available to other citizens is a violation of that person's constitutional rights. This was one basis for Bakke's suit against the UC-Davis medical school's 16 percent minority set-aside for medical school admission. There were eighty-four seats out of the one hundred admission slots that he was eligible to fill, and he was excluded from competing for the other sixteen slots because of his race. On the basis of the standard criteria (GPA, MCAT scores, etc.), Bakke argued that he would have been admitted before any of the Black applicants admitted under the minority set-aside. He therefore claimed that he was being excluded from the additional places available because he was White.

Currently, Blacks have approximately 3.25 times fewer physicians than would be expected given their numbers in the population. Native Americans have 7 times fewer physicians than what would have been expected if intelligent, well-trained, and motivated Native Americans had tried to become physicians at the same rate as did European Americans.

For Fiscus, the underrepresentation of African and Native Americans among physicians and the maldistribution of medical resources to minority communities is clearly the effect of generations of racist exclusions. Because of stereotypes portraying them as the product of cognitive deficiencies, unstable families, bad habits, and inadequate educations, Blacks and Native Americans seeking to obtain educational, employment, and investment opportunities have traditionally been perceived to be less prepared than their White competitors. Not only are qualified members of the oppressed group harmed by this prejudice, but even more harmed are the many who would have been qualified but for injuries induced by racial prejudice.

For Fiscus, individuals of different races would have been as equally distributed in the social body as the molecules of a gas in a container and he identifies the belief in the inherent equality of races with the Equal Protection Clause of the Fourteenth Amendment.[112] In a world without racism, minorities would be represented among the top one hundred medical school applicants at UC-Davis in the same proportion as they were in the general population. Accordingly, because Bakke did not score among the top eighty-four Whites, he would not have qualified for admission. Thus, he had no right to the position he was contesting, and indeed if he were given such a position in lieu of awarding it to a minority, Bakke would be much like a person who had received stolen goods. "Individuals who have not personally harmed minorities may nevertheless be prevented from reaping the benefits of the harm inflicted by the society at large."[113]

Justice O'Connor has voiced skepticism toward the assumption that members of different races would "gravitate with mathematical exactitude to each employer or union absent unlawful discrimination."[114] She considers it sheer speculation as to "how many minority students would have been admitted to the medical school at Davis absent past discrimination in educational opportunities."[115] I likewise consider it speculative to assume that races would be represented in every area in proportion to their proportion of the general population. But because it is impossible to reasonably predict what that distribution would have been absent racial discrimination, it is not mere speculation but morally fair practice to assume that it would have been the same as the proportion in the general population. Given the fact of legally sanctioned invidious racism against Blacks in U.S. history, the burden of proof should not be on the oppressed group to prove that it would be represented at a level proportionate to its presence in the general population. Rather, the burden of proof should be on the majority to show why its overrepresentation among the most well off is not the result of unfair competition imposed by racism. We are morally obligated to assume proportional representation until there are more plausible reasons than racism for assuming otherwise.

Like Fiscus, I believe that races are equal, but that need not imply that they are identical in all relevant respects. Belief in racial equality requires us to acknowledge that racial differences, if they exist, should be allowed opportunities for cultivation free of racist restrictions. Only when opportunities are openly available can natural distributions based on natural differences be determined. In a situation not skewed by racism, Blacks might be more concentrated in certain areas and less concentrated in others. But to accept as the norm that they would be concentrated in the lower echelons of most areas, if represented at all, is racist. Because of the universality of prejudice against Blacks, gross disparities in proportional representation should alert us to the probability that it is caused by racist restrictions rather than racialist differences or personal preferences.

Thus, it should be the responsibility of the Alabama Department of Public Safety to show why no Blacks were members of it's highway patrol as of 1970, even though Blacks were 25 percent of the relevant workforce in Alabama. It should be the responsibility of the company and the union to explain why there were no Blacks with seniority in the union at the Kaiser plant in Louisiana, although Blacks made up 39 percent of the surrounding population. Likewise, it should be the responsibility of the union to explain why no Blacks had been admitted to the Sheet Metal Workers' Union in New York City although minorities were 29 percent of the available workforce. If no alternative explanations are more plausible, then the assumption that the disparity in representation is the result of racism should stand.

The question should not be whether White males are innocent or guilty of racism or sexism, but whether they have a right to inflated odds of obtaining benefits relative to minorities and women. A White male is innocent only up to the point where he takes advantage of "a benefit he would not qualify for without the accumulated effects of racism. At that point he becomes an accomplice in, and a beneficiary of, society's racism. He becomes the recipient of stolen goods."[116]

While Justice Scalia dismisses the racism that may have been practiced by Italians, Irish, and other immigrant groups as insignificant compared to the racism practiced under slavery, it is plausible that racism after slavery was more instrumental in creating the situation that affirmative action was meant to relieve than racism during slavery.[117]

While many European immigrant groups were no more literate than Blacks who were already in America, they were nonetheless granted state support in acquiring property (the Homestead Acts, the FHA, urban renewal), education (the Morrill Act, segregated schools), and jobs (NLRB and governmental support for racist unions) that Blacks were denied. Unions, municipalities, and lending institutions used legally sanctioned means to exclude Blacks from employment, educational, and investment opportunities made available to European immigrants. While union members benefited from government interventions in the labor market as a result of legislation such as the Wagner Act, the National Apprenticeship Act, and the Davis-Bacon Act, they actively practiced nepotism and ethnic preferences in the award of jobs and training.[118]

Certainly the hardships that made Scalia's father flee Italy caused great suffering. The prejudices against illiterate southern European Catholics in a country dominated by northern European protestants were formidable enough to make alternatives such as Argentina and Brazil attractive to many Italian immigrants. But such difficulties do not justify the racist advantages taken by immigrant Europeans on African and Native Americans. Though Scalia's father may have been poor and hard working, neither he nor his progeny should maintain primary rights to benefits that are the result of racist advantages.[119]

On the other hand, Fiscus argues that Whites should not be forced to forgo more than what they arguably would have received in a racially fair society. Because the quotas imposed in *Weber* and *Paradise* exceeded the proportion of Blacks in the relevant populations, they unduly burdened the current generations of White job seekers in order to accelerate opportunities for minorities.

> A disproportional quota violates the rights of nonminority individuals, and a less than proportional quota unfairly rewards nonminority individuals for the society's racism"[120]

As Justice O'Connor wrote in her dissent to *Paradise*:

> protection of the rights of nonminority workers demands that a racial goal not substantially exceed the percentage of minority group members in the relevant population or work force absent compelling justification.

In aiming at proportionality, not as a natural outcome but as a condition necessary to determine natural outcomes, the rights of innocent White males are not being sacrificed for the greater good of increasing the participation of minorities and women. The good of a more diverse society should not be conceived of as justifying the sacrifice of a "randomly chosen" subset of White males currently seeking educational, employment, and entrepreneurial opportunities. Rather, White males are being forced to relinquish benefits that are ill gotten, benefits they would likely not have received in a racially fair world.[121]

Cass Sunstein also argues that the traditional compensation model based on the model of a discrete injury caused by one individual (the tort-feasor or defendant) and suffered by another individual (the plaintiff) is inadequate to capture the situation arising from racial and sexual discrimination.[122] With the traditional tortlike model, the situation exist-ing prior to the injury is assumed to be noncontestable, and the purpose of restitution is to restore the injured party to the position that party would have occupied if the injury had not occurred. But in cases where the injury is not well defined, where neither defendant nor plaintiff are individuals connected by a discrete event, and where the position the injured party would have occupied but for the injury is unspecifiable, then in such cases dependence on the traditional model of compensatory justice is questionable.[123]

In contrast to the position taken by Fiscus, Sunstein argues that the claim that affirmative action and preferential treatment is meant to put individuals in the position they would have occupied had their groups not been subject to racial and sexual discrimination is nonsensical: "What would the world look like if it had been unaffected by past discrimination on the basis of race and sex? . . . the question is unanswerable, not because of the absence of good social science, but because of the obscure epistemological status of the question itself."[124]

Affirmative action must be justified in terms of alternative conceptions of the purpose of legal intervention, and Sunstein recommends instead the notion of "risk management" (intended to offset increased risks faced by a group rather than compensate the injuries suffered by a particular individual) and the "principle of nonsubordination" (whereby measures are taken to reverse a situation in which an irrelevant difference has been transformed by legally sanctioned acts of the state into a social disadvantage). The notion of risk management is meant to apply to cases where injuries are "individually small but collectively large" so that pursuing each case individually would be too costly both in terms of time and effort.[125] In such cases, those harmed may be unable to establish a direct causal link between their injuries and the plaintiff's actions. Thus, a person who develops a certain type of cancer associated with a toxin produced by a particular company might have developed that condition even in the absence of the company's negligent behavior. At most, they can argue that the company's actions caused an increased risk of injury, rather than any specific instance of that injury.

Harms suffered in this way systemically affect certain groups with higher frequency than other groups, without it being possible to establish causal links between the injuries of specific plaintiffs and the actions of the defendant. Regulatory agencies should be designed to address harms that are the result of increased risks rather than of a discrete action.[126] One of their principle aims should be not to compensate each injured party (and only injured parties), "but instead to deter and punish the risk-creating behavior" by redistributing social goods from the plaintiff to the class of defendants.[127]

The principle of nonsubordination is meant to apply to cases where the existing distribution of wealth and opportunities between groups are the result of law rather than natural attributes.[128] The purpose of affirmative action from a forward-looking perspective should be to end social subordination and reverse the situation in which irrelevant differences have been, through social and legal structures, turned into systematic disadvantages operative in multiple spheres that diminish participation in democratic forms of life.[129]

"Innocent White males" are harmed primarily by being deprived of benefits they would normally expect to acquire. But taking existing inequalities as the baseline for determining violations of equal opportunity implies that the inflated odds against success suffered by those who have been the object of racism and sexism should be accepted as the norm. Given such,

> affirmative action does not appear an impermissible 'taking' of an antecedent entitlement. Because the existing distribution of benefits and burdens between Blacks and Whites and men and women is not natural . . . and because it is in part a product of current laws and practices having discriminatory effects, it is not decisive if some Whites and men are disadvantaged as a result.[130]

A central question in the debate over affirmative action is the extent to which racial classifications are important in accomplishing the goal of relieving the subordinate status of minorities and women. Given the aim of improving safety in transportation, classifying people in terms of their race is rationally irrelevant, while classifying them in terms of their driving competency, visual acuity, and maturity is essential. On the other hand, given the aim of improving health care in Black neighborhoods, classifying applicants for medical school in terms of their race is, in addition to their academic and clinical abilities, a very relevant factor.

To illustrate, African Americans, Hispanics, and Native Americans make up 22 percent of the population but represent only 10 percent of entering medical students and 7 percent of practicing physicians. A number of studies have shown that underrepresented minority physicians are more likely than their majority counterparts to care for poor patients and patients of similar ethnicity. Indeed, "each ethnic group of patients was more likely to be cared for by a physician of their own ethnic background than by a physician of another ethnic background."[131] This suggests that sociocultural factors such as language, physical identity, personal background, and experiences are relevant factors in determining the kinds of communities in which a physician will establish a practice. If this is the case, then the race of a medical school applicant would be an important factor in providing medical services to certain underrepresented communities. Thus, while there might be some purposes for which race is irrelevant, there might be other purposes in which race is important (though perhaps not necessary) for achieving the end in view.[132] The remedy targets Blacks as a group because racially discriminatory practices were directed against Blacks as a group.[133]

Some argue that characteristics such as race, sex, and social background are morally irrelevant because an individual has no choice as to whether such attributes shall attach to him or her. But an individual has no choice about whether he or she will be born with a high IQ or not. Yet, we do not advocate eliminating intellectual potential as a criteria for receiving scarce educational opportunities. Individuals with high IQ are valued because we believe that such individuals play an important role in increasing aggregate wealth. To the extent that we want our society to be a productive one, we allocate special places to such individuals.

A similar rationale holds in the case of race. To the extent that we want our society to be not only productive, but also just, to that extent is it important to demonstrate a concern for those who face decreased opportunities because of racism. Preferential treatment programs are meant to offset the disadvantages imposed by racism so that Blacks are not forced to bear the principal costs of that error.

It is commonly objected that proportionate representation achieved in this manner is artificial. But barriers that exclude Blacks from educational, employment, and entrepreneurial opportunities impose and maintain an artificial underrepresentation. To condemn policies meant to correct for racial barriers as themselves erecting barriers is to ignore the difference between action and reaction, cause and effect, aggression and self-defense. Even a critic of affirmative action such as Robert Fullinwider admits that "If equal opportunity is looked at as some kind of equilibrium, then we can see nothing amiss about tampering with a situation that has got into disequilibrium. We add and subtract weights here and there until equilibrium is restored."[134] Clearly, granting preferential treatment to individuals who suffer the present burdens of discrimination is exactly the kind of tampering that is appropriate.

Conclusion

Racism was directed against Blacks whether they were talented, average, or mediocre, and attenuating the effects of racism requires distributing remedies similarly. Affirmative action policies compensate for the harms of racism (overt and institutional) through antidiscrimination laws and preferential policies. Prohibiting the benign use of race as a factor in the award of educational, employment and business opportunities would eliminate compensation for past and present racism and reinforce the moral validity of the status quo, with Blacks overrepresented among the least well off and underrepresented among the most well off.

It has become popular to use affirmative action as a scapegoat for the increased vulnerability of the White working class. But it should be recognized that the civil rights revolution (in general) and affirmative action (in particular) has been beneficial, not just to Blacks, but also to Whites (e.g., women, the disabled, the elderly) who otherwise would be substantially more vulnerable than they are now.

Affirmative action is directed toward empowering those groups that have been adversely affected by past and present exclusionary practices. Initiatives to abolish preferential treatment would inflict a grave injustice on African Americans, for they signal a reluctance to acknowledge that the plight of African Americans is the result of institutional practices that require institutional responses.

Notes

1. Kent Greenawalt, *Discrimination and Reverse Discrimination* (New York: Alfred A. Knopf, 1983), 129 ff.

2. Kathanne W. Greene, *Affirmative Action and Principles of Justice* (New York: Greenwood Press, 1989), 22.

3. Kennedy stated: "even the complete elimination of racial discrimination in employment—a goal toward which this nation must strive—will not put a single unemployed Negro to work unless he has the skills required." Greene, *Affirmative Action*, 23.

4. Greene, *Affirmative Action*, 31.

5. Greene, *Affirmative Action*, 41.

6. Greene, *Affirmative Action*, 40.

7. Representatives Willis (D-La.), Forrester (D-Ga.), Tuck (D-Va.), Ashmore (D-S.C.), Dowdy (D-Miss.), and Whitener (D-N.C.) (Greene, *Affirmative Action*, 29).

8. Greene, *Affirmative Action*, 54.

9. Nicolaus Mills (ed.), *Debating Affirmative Action* (New York: Dell Publishing, 1994), 10–12.

10. Greenawalt, *Discrimination*, 160–62.

11. Chief Justice Burger, *Griggs v. Duke Power Co.*, 401 US at 429,230; Greene, *Affirmative Action*, 64.

12. Suppose the practice selects 75 percent of applicants from group B and 50 percent of the applicants from group A. Since 4/5 of 75 percent is 60 percent and the practice only selects 50 percent of applicants from A, the practice has an adverse impact on group A.

13. Mills, *Debating Affirmative Action*, 14.

14. Derrick Bell, *And We Are Not Saved*, (New York: Basic Books, 1987); see also, Gertrude Ezorsky's *Racism and Justice* (Ithica, N.Y.: Cornell University Press,1991) [on recruitment by personal networks] and John Larew's "Who's the Real Affirmative Action Profiteer" in *The Washington Monthly*, June 1991 [admission to elite schools based on parental alumni status].

15. Bell, *And We Are Not Saved*, chap. 2, "The Benefits to Whites of Civil Rights Litigation."

16. As in *Albermarle Paper Co. v. Moody* (1975); see Greene, *Affirmative Action*, 67 ff.

17. *Franks v. Bowman Transportation Co.* (1976); *International Brotherhood of Teamsters v. United States* (1977); Greene, *Affirmative Action*, 65–70.

18. 438 US at 307; Greene, *Affirmative Action*, 73–74.

19. 438 US at 363; Greene, *Affirmative Action*, 75.

20. Governmental complicity would include slavery and legally mandated differential treatment that deprived Blacks of educational, employment, and investment opportunities made available to Whites.

21. 438 US at 407; Greene, *Affirmative Action*, 77.

22. Greene, *Affirmative Action*, 79.

23. See Drew Days III (1987), "Fullilove" in Yale Law Journal, 96: 461–62 for past history of discrimination by Kaiser and United Steelworkers. By entering into a voluntary agreement to end discriminatory practices, both union and

employer could avoid costly suits for back pay and promotions that might result from an official finding of discrimination.

24. Brief for Kaiser, No. 78–432:40–42; Greene, *Affirmative Action*, 88–89.

25. 443 US at 208; Greene, *Affirmative Action*, 92.

26. Mills, *Debating Affirmative Action*, 19.

27. Brief for Petitioner, No.84–1340:11; Greene, *Affirmative Action*, 108–109.

28. Brief for the US, No.84–1340:25–26, n.42; Greene, *Affirmative Action*, 109.

29. The same would apply for Title VI and voluntary compliance by educational institutions.

30. It was clearly intended by the Congress that the Civil Rights Act encourage voluntary compliance.

31. 476 US at 306; Greene, *Affirmative Action*, 115.

32. See Julius Jacobson, "Union Conservatism: A Barrier to Racial Equality" in *The Negro and the American Labor Movement* (New York: Doubleday Anchor, 1968) for an elaboration of the thesis that the American working class has long been violently racist. With regard to the above incident, Jacobson writes: "on the one hand, they argue that one reason Negroes are not found in the craft unions is that they do not have the skills; on the other hand, when Negroes prove that they do have the skills, it is argued that they must have cheated" (20–21).

33. Amicus Brief for City of Birmingham, No.84–1656:24; Greene, *Affirmative Action*, 124.

34. 478 US at 474; Greene, *Affirmative Action*, 126–127.

35. 478 US at 478; Greene, *Affirmative Action*, 127.

36. Brief for Respondent, Vanguards, No. 84–1999:35; Greene, *Affirmative Action*, 133.

37. *NAACP v. Allen*, 480 US at 156; Greene, *Affirmative Action*, 138.

38. Establishing prior discrimination without need of specifying individual cases would avoid exposing the agency to suits from the individuals identified.

39. 107 Supreme Court at 1459; Greene, *Affirmative Action*, 153.

40. Mills, *Debating Affirmative Action*, 20.

41. Mills, *Debating Affirmative Action*, 25–26.

42. Of course, requiring a direct causal link would eliminate the possibility of claiming that cigarette smoke was the cause of increased occurrences of cancer or heart disease. Some people who smoke do not contract cancer or have heart disease, and some people who get cancer or contract heart disease do not smoke.

It is on this basis that Justice Clarence Thomas argued (in *Helling v. McKinney, 1993*) that a prisoner forced to share a cell with another who smoked five packs of cigarettes a day was not subject to unnecessary punishment, because, in Justice Thomas' opinion, injury could not consist of increased risk but must be the direct result of a specific act or condition. (see remarks by Judge A. Leon Higginbotham, *Black Issues in Higher Education*, 7 April 1994, 13) But just as there is no direct link between second-hand smoke and cancer, likewise there is no direct link between the low participation of MBEs in government business and past racism.

For more on this, see the distinction between atomistic and ecological causation in Michael Rosenfeld, *Affirmative Action and Justice* (New Haven: Yale University Press, 1991), 211.

43. *New York Times,* 13 June 1995, D24.

44. Excerpts from *Adarand Constructors v. Pena* in New York Times, 13 June 1995, D24.

45. New York Times, 13 June 1995, D24; As to whether we are all "one race" in America, see Andrew Hacker, *Two Nations: Black and White, Separate, Hostile, Unequal* (New York: Ballantine Books, 1995).

46. *New York Times,* 13 June 1995, D24.

47. *New York Times,* 13 June 1995, D24.

48. Bernard Boxill, "The Morality of Reparation" in *Social Theory and Practice,* 2, no.1, Spring 1972: 118–119. It is for such reasons that welfare programs are not sufficient to satisfy the claims of Blacks for restitution. Welfare programs contain no admission of the unjust violation of rights and seek merely to provide the basic means for all to pursue opportunities in the future.

49. I am presuming that most of us would recognize certain primae facie duties such as truth telling, promise keeping, restitution, benevolence, justice, nonmalficience as generally obligatory. See W. D. Ross, *The Right and the Good* (Oxford: Clarendon Press, 1930).

50. Even in the case where y was only as qualified as z, a fair method of choice between candidates should produce an equitable distribution of such positions between Blacks and Whites in the long run if not in the short.

51. Judith Jarvis Thompson, *Philosophy and Public Affairs* 2, (Summer 1973):379–380.

52. *Sheet Metal Workers v. EEOC* (1986); *United States v. Paradise* (1987).

53. Thomas Sowell, *Ethnic America* (New York: Basic Books, 1981); *Preferential Policies: An International Perspective* (New York: William Morrow, 1990); For a recent critique of Sowell's position, see Christopher Jencks, *Rethinking Social Policy: Race Poverty, and the Underclass,* (New York: Harper, 1993), chap. 1.

54. Michael Levin, "Race, Biology, and Justice" in *Public Affairs Quarterly,* 8, no.3 (July 1994). There are many good reasons for skepticism regarding the validity of using IQ as a measure of cognitive ability. See *The Bell Curve Wars* ed. Steven Fraser (New York: Basic Books, 1995); *The Bell Curve Debate* ed. by Russell Jacoby and Naomi Glauberman (New York: Times Books, 1995); Allan Chase, *The Legacy of Malthus* (Urbana: University of Illinois Press, 1980); Steven J. Gould, *The Mismeasure of Man* (New York: Norton, 1981); R.C. Lewontin, S.Rose, L.J. Kamin, *Not In Our Genes,* (New York:Pantheon Books, 1984).

55. See Robert Fullinwider, *The Reverse Discrimination Controversy: A Moral and Legal Analysis,* (Totowa, N.J.: Rowman & Littlefield, 1980), 117. Ronald Fiscus, *The Constitutional Logic of Affirmative Action* (Durham, N.C.: Duke University Press, 1992).

56. Fullinwider, *Reverse Discrimination Controversy,* 55; also Alan Goldman, "Reparations to Individuals or Groups?" *Analysis* 35 (April 1975):168–170.

57. Ellen Frankel Paul, "Set-Asides, Reparations, and Compensatory Justice"

in *Nomos* 33, *Compensatory Justice*, ed. by John Chapman (New York: New York University Press, 1991), 106–7; for Justice Stevens' dissent, see *Fullilove v. Klutznick*(1980) 448 U.S. at 552.

58. Alan Goldman, "Reparations to Individuals or Groups?", *Analysis*, 35, no.1, (April 1975):169. Even ardent defenders of preferential treatment as a form of reparation such as Bernard Boxill have tended to accept without qualification the view that Blacks who are most qualified have been harmed least by racist exclusions. While granting this assumption, Boxill argues that qualified Blacks have been harmed, even if not as badly as those who are unqualified, and are therefore deserving of compensation: "Because I have lost only one leg, I may be less deserving of compensation than another who has lost two legs, but it does not follow that I deserve no compensation at all." *Blacks and Social Justice* (Totowa, N.J.: Rowman & Littlefield, 1984), 148.

59. Christopher Jencks, *Rethinking Social Policy*, (New York: Harper, 1993), 51–52.

60. John Ogbu, *Minority Education and Caste*, (New York: Academic Press, 1978), 175.

61. Again, I am not suggesting that people without qualifications are not harmed by racial discrimination. But they would be harmed even in the absence of racial discrimination. Nor am I suggesting that people who lack qualifications have less intellectual potential. I am claiming that a person with above average ability to do R is harmed more by being deprived of the opportunity to reap the benefits of doing R than one with average or below average ability to do R. At the extreme, a person lacking the ability to do R would be injured minimally by being deprived of the opportunity to do R. And one with exceptional ability to do R would be deprived maximally.

62. In general, I would argue that if y is talented with respect to ability r and ordinary with respect to ability s, then depriving y of r is a greater harm than depriving y of s. Likewise, depriving Blacks of the opportunity to develop and exercise intellectual and leadership capacities imposes a greater harm on those with high potential in those areas than on those Blacks with average or low potential in those respects. This argument would apply equally to women. Boxill recognizes a similar point when he writes: "if thugs break the basketball player Dr. J's legs, he will receive more compensation than I would if they broke my legs, because it is known that his legs are a greater asset to him than are my legs to me." Boxill, *Blacks and Social Justice* 154.

63. It is testimony to the conservative nature of affirmative action that it does not attempt to rectify the disadvantages of class discrimination that is an inherent part of a capitalist economy. Yet many seem to criticize affirmative action for not addressing the needs of those who are victims, not merely of racial discrimination, but of the vagaries of a constantly changing competitive economy.

64. Lester Thurow, "A Theory of Groups and Economic Redistribution," *Philosophy and Public Policy*,9, no.1 (1979):29.

65. Owen Fiss, "Groups and the Equal Protection Clause," *Philosophy and Public Affairs*, 5, no.2 (winter 1976):107–177.

66. Fiss, "Groups," 160.

67. As Virginia Held puts it: There is no doubt at all that it would be better to get a job or promotion or a school admission based on unbiased judgment that one deserves it rather than through the pressure exerted by affirmative action programs. . . . [But] given continuing discrimination, is it better for women and minority members to face the slurs and innuendos from the position of having a job or promotion or a degree, or to face comparable slurs and innuendos about a lack of competence or merit from the position of not having the job or the promotion or the degree? *Dissent* (Fall 1995):467.

68. Fiss, "Groups," 173.

69. Paul, "Set-Asides, Reparations, and Compensatory Justice" *Nomos* 33, ed. Michael Chapman (New York: New York Univ. Press, 1991):97–139. See also Christopher Morris, "Existential Limits to the Rectification of Past Wrongs" in *American Philosophical Quarterly*, 21, no.2 (April 1984).

70. Paul, "Set-Asides," 119.

71. Michael Levin, "Is Racial Discrimination Special?" in *Journal of Value Inquiry* 15 (1981):232.

72. An analogous argument would be that had Jane not been raped by John, the child, y, resulting from that rape (and, let us assume for the sake of symmetry, now living with John) would have been born under the even worse conditions that Jane subsequently experienced. But clearly, it is plausible that had Jane not been raped, she would not have become as bad off as she became after having been raped. And the child, y, born of the rape would have been neither worse off nor better off had it been born under different conditions, since y would not exist other than under the conditions it was actually born under. But it does not follow that Jane would have had no children had she not been raped, though y would not exist had she not been raped. It may be true that y was born into circumstances that are much worse than the circumstances under which Jane would have had a child voluntarily. This does not mean that y is worse off than y otherwise would have been, since y otherwise would not have existed. Y could not therefore claim compensation from John on the ground that it would have been better off if it had been born under more fortuitous circumstances. But y could claim compensation if, after it was born, it was taken and systematically exploited by John (y's father). And Jane may certainly be worse off as a result of having to give birth under such circumstances.

73. For a discussion of this and similar issues relating to the notion of wrongful life, see James S. Fishkin, "Justice Between Generations" *Nomos*, 33 ed. by John Chapman (New York: New York University Press, 1991):85–96. See also David Heyd, *Genethics-Moral Issues in the Creation of People* (Berkeley: University of California Press, 1992): chaps. 1 and 4.

74. Paul, "Set-Asides," 129.

75. Paul, "Set-Asides," 129.

76. See Alfred W. Blumrosen quoting Justice Marshall that, given the enormous power that government holds over the lives of citizens, "government refusal

to act could have just as devastating an effect upon life, liberty, and the pursuit of happiness as coercive governmental action" in "Society in Transition IV: Affirmation of Affirmative Action under the Civil Rights Act of 1991," *Rutgers Law Review* 45, no.4 (Summer 1993):904.

77. For a survey of these issues, see Vincene Verdun, "If the Shoe Fits, Wear It: An Analysis of Reparations to African Americans," *Tulane Law Revue* 67, no.3 (Feb.1993):597–668.

78. This is a point that has been made again and again by Bernard Boxill in "The Morality of Preferential Treatment," *Philosophy and Public Affairs* 7, no.3 (Spring 1978):246–268; *Blacks and Social Justice* (Totowa, N.J.:Rowman & Littlefield, 1984), chap. 7; and "Equality, Discrimination, and Preferential Treatment" in *A Companion to Ethics* ed. Peter Singer (Cambridge: Blackwell, 1993).

79. Orlando Patterson, *Slavery and Social Death* (Cambridge: Harvard University Press, 1982), 260.

80. Patterson concludes: "Enslavement, slavery, and manumission are not merely related events; they are one and the same process in different phases." *Slavery*, 296.

81. Paul Hoffman in *Reverse Discrimination* ed. Barry Gross (Buffalo, N.Y.:Prometheus Books, 1977), 368.

82. That many with high potential would have been denied opportunities to develop their potential because of class exclusions is not to be denied. What I deny is that racial and class discrimination are identical. It is indicative of the conservative nature of affirmative action that it does not address class discrimination.

83. See Boxill at note 11.

84. Glenn Loury, *One by One from the Inside Out: Essays and Reviews on Race and Responsibility in America* (New York: Free Press, 1995).

85. Loury, *One by One*, 103; for a similar treatment of the importance of personal connections, see Gertrude Ezorsky, *Racism and Justice* (Ithica, N.Y.: Cornell University Press, 1991), 14ff.

86. Loury, *One by One*, 106.

87. Loury, *One by One*, 107.

88. Loury, *One by One*, 110.

89. It is important to note that, far from being the vision of socialist revolutionaries, strong affirmative action is a conservative response to racial injustice. It does not seek to eliminate the growing gap between rich and poor. Rather, it seeks to eliminate the overrepresentation of Blacks among the least well off and their underrepresentation among the most well off. It addresses the growth of underclass only in the sense that Blacks should not be a greater proportion of this class than other racial groups. It does not create new jobs. Rather, it addresses how jobs already created shall be distributed.

90. See Andrew Hacker, *Two Nations* (New York: Ballantine, 1992), 118.

91. Hacker, *Two Nations*, 126.

92. Gary Becker, *The Economics of Discrimination* (Chicago: University of Chicago Press, 1971).

93. For a discussion of this see Robert Fogel, *Without Consent or Contract: The Rise and Fall of American Slavery* (New York: Norton, 1989), 393ff.

94. See *New York Times,* 1 Febuary 1995, A12, for sexual harassment suit against the FBI; see *New York Times,* 25 Febuary 1994, A12, for class action suit by five hundred Black employees of the Immigration Service. Major retailers include AT&T, Sears, and Denny's. See *New York Times,* 30 March 1995, B6 reporting settlement setting target for *New York Times* and the New York Newspaper Printing Pressmen's Union No. 2 to hire 25 percent minorities and women over the next ten years."The consent decree affects free lance applicants who show up at the *Times'* Manhattan plant . . . applying to mop floors, clean printing machines, move stacks of compacted papers and perform other odd jobs. . . . In 1992 the union had no Blacks, Asians or women" and "the casuals pool consisted entirely of White men, except for one person at the bottom of the list."

95. Lawrence Kahn and Peter Sherer, "Racial Differences in Professional Basketball Players' Compensation," *Journal of Labor Economics* 6 (1988):40–61; Clark Nardinella and Curtis Simon, "Customer Racial Discrimination in the Market for Memorabilia: The Case of Baseball" in *The Quarterly Journal of Economics* 105, no.3 (August 1990):575–95.

96. "Fair Driving: Gender and Race Discrimination in Retail Car Negotiations" by Ian Ayres in *Harvard Law Review* 104 (Febuary 1991) no.4:817–72.

97. *New York Times,* 13 July 1995, D1. A similar pattern was reported in Ohio, where it was reported that Blacks were turned down at twice the rate of similarly qualified white applicants. See Columbus Dispatch, 14 February 1995, 4c, report by Ohio commerce director Nancy Chiles.

98. Margery Turner, Michael Fix, and Raymond Struyk, *Opportunities Denied, Opportunities Diminished:Racial Discrimination in Hiring,* (Washington, D.C.: The Urban Institute Press, 1991), 2. The authors conclude: "In sum, when equally qualified black and white candidates competed for a job, differential treatment, when it occurred, was three times more likely to favor the white applicant than the black."

99. *New York Times,* 25 March 1994, 19.

100. See David Goldberg, *Racist Culture* (Cambridge, Mass.: Blackwell, 1993).

101. Jencks concludes that "For the foreseeable future, many different firms will stand to gain economically from discrimination, and unless the government is active in discouraging such practices, they will persist." *Rethinking Social Policy,* 69.

102. As with Justice Stevens' comments.

103. Of course, we are likely to draw the line in the case where x has intentionally deprived y of a basic need. In such case, we would likely insist that x's obligation to make restitution would supercede any rights x may have to provide himself or others with basic necessities.

104. Boxill has argued that examples such as this are misleading, for ideally we should conceive of preferential treatment as making it possible for advantaged Blacks to compete for positions that otherwise would be filled by advantaged Whites, and disadvantaged Blacks to compete for positions that otherwise would

be filled by disadvantaged Whites. (See Boxill, *Blacks and Social Justice*, 161ff.) But we must be careful in using income as a the primary criteria for determining social advantage. On the average, a middle-class Black person making $60,000 a year has less capital (in terms of real property and financial assets) than a lower class White person making $16,000 a year. It is plausible that many poor Whites have an equal excess of human capital to draw on as well. (See Melvin Oliver and Thomas Shapiro, *Black Wealth/White Wealth*, (New York: Routledge, 1995), chap. 5.)

105. Likewise, in the case of many poor Blacks, the injuries of class may surpass the injuries of race. But this does not mean that injuries of race are nonexistent.

106. In this sense, graduating Blacks from medical school who are unqualified to practice medicine would be more a disadvantage than advantage to the patients they are most likely to serve.

107. Ronald J. Fiscus, *The Constitutional Logic of Affirmative Action* (Durham, N.C.: Duke University Press, 1992).

108. Scalia, "Commentary—The Disease as Cure," 1979 *Washington University Law Quarterly*, 147, at 152 (quoted in Fiscus, *Constitutional Logic*, 12).

109. Richard Posner, "The DeFunis Case," 16 (quoted in Fiscus, *Constitutional Logic*, 12).

110. Fiscus, *Constitutional Logic*, 13.

111. Unless it is necessary for (strict scrutiny) or contributes toward (intermediate scrutiny) the achievement of an important social goal.

112. Fiscus, *Constitutional Logic*, 20–26.

113. Fiscus, *Constitutional Logic*, 38.

114. *Sheet Metal Workers v. EEOC*, 478 US 421, 494 (1986); Fiscus, *Constitutional Logic*, 42.

115. *City of Richmond v. J.A. Croson Co.*, 109 S.Ct. at 724 (1989); Fiscus, *Constitutional Logic*, 42.

116. Fiscus, *Constitutional Logic*, 47. With regard to the problem of so-called "undeserving beneficiaries" of affirmative action Fiscus writes: "When the rightful owner of stolen goods cannot be found, the law . . . may or may not award possession to the original but wrongful claimant; but if it does not, if it awards possession to a third party whose claim is arguable, the original claimant cannot justifiably feel morally harmed. And the government's action cannot be said to be arbitrary unless it awards the goods to an individual whose claim is even less plausible than that of the original claimant." (49).

117. See J. Owens Smith, *The Politics of Racial Inequality* (New York: Greenwood Press, 1987): "The cause of the present-day income inequality among Blacks can be attributed not to what happened to them during slavery, but to what happened to them from the passage of the National Labor Relations Act in 1935 to the implementation of affirmative action. . . . The NLRA gave labor unions the exclusive power . . . to allocate skilled jobs in those sectors that produced high income to members of their own groups . . . this act gave unions exclusive control over who could and could not enter the skilled trades. . . . The Unions used this power to exclude Blacks from the mainstream of society's income redistribution system." (156, 157).

118. The Wagner Act established the National Labor Relations Board giving unions the power to bargain for employees. The National Apprenticeship Act established apprenticeship programs subsidized by the federal government. Dominated by the unions, this program excluded Blacks. The Bacon-Davis Act required employers with government contracts to pay union wages even though unions systematically excluded Blacks (J. Owens Smith, *The Politics of Racial Inequality*, 160–65).

119. I agree with Fiscus that "unfairness to poor whites is a serious matter in its own right—so serious that one cannot say that it is a lesser injustice than racial injustice. But the point is that it is a different injustice, and the net unfairness of the society is not improved by giving to poor whites what blacks would have won under racially fair conditions" (Fiscus, *Constitutional Logic*, 50).

120. Fiscus, *Constitutional Logic*, 62.

121. "There is no discrimination against the innocent white individuals involved, and hence no constitutional violation of equal protection". (Fiscus, *Constitutional Logic*, 84).

122. Cass Sunstein, "The Limits of Compensatory Justice" in *Nomos* 33, *Compensatory Justice*, ed. John Chapman (New York: New York University Press, 1991), 281–310.

123. "It is not controlling and perhaps not even relevant that the harms that affirmative action attempts to redress cannot be understood in the usual compensatory terms. . . . the nature of the problem guarantees that the legal response cannot take the form of discrete remedies for discrete harms" (Sunstein, "Limits," 297).

124. Sunstein, "Limits," 303.

125. The orientation of the EEOC toward investigating individual cases of alleged discrimination is one explanation of its extraordinary backlog of over 80,000 cases. This orientation precludes it from focusing on systemic practices that affect many individuals, and instead forces it to expend resources dealing with particular instances. See "The EEOC: Pattern and Practice Imperfect" by Maurice Munroe in *Yale Law and Policy Review*, 13, no.2, (1995):219–80.

126. Sunstein, "Limits," 292.

127. Sunstein, "Limits," 289.

128. "The current distribution of benefits and burdens as between blacks an whites and women and men is not part of the state of nature but a consequence of past and present social practices" (Sunstein, "Limits," 294).

129. See also Thomas H. Simon, *Democracy and Social Injustice* (Lanham, Md.: Rowman & Littlefield, 1995), chap.5.

130. Sunstein, "Limits," 306.

131. Gang Xu, Sylvia Fields, et al. "The Relationship between the Ethnicity of Generalist Physicians and Their Care for Underserved Populations," Ohio University College of Osteopathic Medicine, Athens, Ohio, 10.

132. Of course, we may ask whether the use of race is necessary for the achievement of the end in view or whether it is one among alternative ways of

achieving that end. For instance, it might be possible to induce doctors to practice in Black neighborhoods by providing doctors, irrespective of their race, with suitable monetary incentives. But given the importance of nonmonetary factors in physician-patient relationships, it is doubtful that purely monetary rewards would be sufficient to meet the needs of underserved populations.

133. Remedial action based on the imbalance between blacks in the available work force and their presence in skilled jobs categories presumes that imbalance is caused by racial discrimination. This assumption has been challenged by many who cite cultural and cognitive factors that might equally be the cause of such imbalances. See Thomas Sowell, *Markets and Minorities* (New York: Basic Books, 1981); Richard Herrenstein and Charles Murray, *The Bell Curve* (New York: The Free Press, 1994). This literature has itself been subject to critique: for Sowell, see Christopher Jencks, *Rethinking Social Policy*, (New York: Harper, 1993); for Herrenstein and Murray, see *The Bell Curve Wars*, ed. Steven Fraser (New York: Basic Books, 1995).

134. Fullinwider, *Reverse Discrimination*, 117.

equalizing access to resources and bringing people together so as to overcome stereotypes. However, despite all of these changes, too many African Americans remain dysfunctional. In fact, there is some evidence that many if not most of the programs inaugurated with the Civil Rights Act of 1964 have actually exacerbated the dysfunction.[3]

Affirmative action is the name of a series of initiatives introduced by the civil rights movement and intended to do what previous public policies had not done, that is, allow African Americans to participate more fully in American life.

What Is Affirmative Action?

There is no generally accepted definition of affirmative action. This tells us a number of things. First, any discussion of whether it is a good or a bad thing will turn on what one understands this expression to mean.

Let us take one example of a definition. "Affirmative action is the name given to a number of policies designed to overcome past and present discrimination and provide opportunity for those traditionally denied it."[4] In this sample definition we can distinguish among (1) the policy or set of practices to be instituted—none of which are specifically mentioned; (2) the intention behind the policy—the quite laudable one of expanding opportunities for those who have not had them; and (3) the explicit diagnosis of why those opportunities were not there—the presumption that discrimination is the exclusive or major reason for the lack of opportunity.

Any debate about whether one is for or against affirmative action must specify whether one agrees or disagrees with (2) the intention or goal, (1) policies designed to achieve that goal, and (3) the definition and diagnosis of the problem to which one is applying both the goal and the policies. There are at least three major responses to the foregoing definition:

One might approve of the intention but believe that the policies, will not achieve the intention. This becomes a debate about the best means of achieving a commonly agreed upon goal.

One might approve of the intention but believe that although the policies will achieve their goal, the policies will also conflict with and undermine other socially important goals. This becomes a debate about prioritizing our goals in a world where it is not possible to have everything.

One might approve of the intention but disapprove of the policies because we disagree with the diagnosis. This becomes a debate about what is the nature and source of the problem to which affirmative action as a policy is addressed.

Lack of a generally agreed upon definition also reflects a lack of consensus on the legal and moral status of the concept. The use of the expression is now so widespread that many are apt to presume that there is some firm foundation in law, in morality, or in public policy for it. Among the things that the ongoing debate about affirmative action has revealed are both the ignorance of and the disagreement about the moral, legal, and political principles that inform or should inform public policy. Perhaps the most useful thing that will come out of a debate about affirmative action is that it will require us, as a society, to refocus on our fundamental principles.

Five major definitions of affirmative action exist:

Definition 1 (open-search): Affirmative action consists of those policies designed to advertise all openings as widely as possible and to monitor appointments and promotions processes in order to insure that the process is open, nondiscriminatory, and promotes excellence.

Definition 2 (punitive): Affirmative action consists of any policy, private or public, *ordered by the court* to redress proven cases of individual discrimination. The remedy may involve a specific *numerical objective*, but the numerical objective is limited to a specific time and place.

Definition 3 (minority set-asides): Affirmative action refers to congressionally mandated rules concerning federal contracts and involving a specific percentage of contracts to be set aside for minority contractors.

Definition 4 (backward-compensation): Affirmative action covers any policy designed to redress alleged cases of discrimination against a group by placing members of the group in the positions they would have allegedly held if the alleged discrimination had not taken place. This is a *contrary-to-fact conditional*: it claims to identify what would happen *if* something else had *not* happened.

Definition 5 (forward-preferential): Affirmative action designates any policy in social planning, without any causal claim of what would have been, designed to produce a society or institution that reflects some stated goal and invokes *quotas* of group representation.[5]

Affirmative Action Is Illegal

Affirmative action in anything other than the most innocuous sense is illegal. Affirmative action in the senses of definitions 1, 2, and 3 (in a highly limited version) is legal. Affirmative action in the senses of definitions 4 and 5 is illegal. There are five reasons for this.

First, according to the Fourteenth Amendment to the United States Constitution, no state can "deprive any person of life, liberty, or property, without due process of law; nor deny to any person within its jurisdiction the equal protection of the laws." This amendment makes clear that it is individuals, not groups, who have rights.

The first relevant use of the expression "affirmative action" appears in an executive order issued in September 1965 by then President Lyndon B. Johnson requiring federal contractors to take "affirmative action to ensure that applicants are employed, and that employees are treated during employment, without regard to their race, creed, color, or national origin." This is an executive order, not a legislative decision and not a decision of the United States Supreme Court; what it makes explicit is the anti-discrimination principles that are already in the law (thereby encompassing definition 1); curiously, sex and gender are not mentioned.

Second, Titles VI and VII of the Civil Rights Act of 1964 unequivocally outlaw preference (definition 5). Two provisions spell this out:

> 703 (h) it shall not be unlawful employment practice . . . for an employer to give and act upon the results of any professionally developed ability test provided that such test, its administration or action upon the results is not designed, intended or used to discriminate because of race, color, religion, sex or national origin. . . .

> 703 (j) Nothing contained in this title shall be interpreted to require any employer . . . to grant preferential treatment to any individual or to any group because of the race, color, religion, sex, or national origin of such individual or group on account of an imbalance which may exist with respect to the total number of percentage of persons of any race, color, religion, sex or national origin employed by any employer.

Lest there be any misunderstanding about these provisions, it is useful to cite the legislative record concerning them. As then Senator Hubert H. Humphrey put it, "Title VII does not require an employer to achieve any sort of racial balance in his work force by giving preferential treatment to any individual or group."[6] Senator Harrison Williams noted that Title VII "specifically prohibits the Attorney General or any agency of the government, from requiring employment to be on the basis of racial or religious quotas. Under this provision an employer with only white employees could continue to have only the best qualified persons even if they were all white."[7] Senator Joseph Clark stated, "Quotas are themselves discriminatory."[8] If anyone still has any doubts, then recall the words of Representative Emanuel Celler, Chairman of the House Judiciary Committee and the congressman responsible for introducing the legislation:

> It is likewise not true that the Equal Employment Opportunity Commission would have power to rectify existing 'racial or religious imbalance' in employment by requiring the hiring of certain people without regard to their qualifications simply because they are of a given race or religion. Only actual discrimination could be stopped.[9]

Third, in *Griggs v. Duke Power Co.* (1971), the U.S. Supreme Court went out of its way to disclaim preference.

> Congress did not intend . . . to guarantee a job to every person regardless of qualifications . . . [Title VII] does not command that any person be hired simply because he was formerly the subject of discrimination, or because he is a member of a minority group. Discriminatory preference for any group, minority or majority, is precisely and only what Congress has proscribed. . . . Congress has not commanded that the less qualified be preferred over the better qualified simply because of minority origins. Far from disparaging job qualifications as such, Congress has made such qualifications the controlling factor, so that race, religion, nationality, and sex become irrelevant."[10]

Fourth, in the pivotal *Alan Bakke* case (1978), Justice Powell, in the plurality opinion, specifically attacked and rejected the backward-looking argument for compensation (what I have called definition 4). To begin with, Justice Powell reiterated that the law and previous U.S. Supreme Court decisions were directed toward overt instances of discrimination: "we have never approved preferential classifications in the absence of proven constitutional or statutory violations." In addition, the overt instances of discrimination can only be recognized as directed toward individuals: "We have never approved a classification that aids persons perceived as members of relatively victimized groups at the expense of other innocent individuals." In specifically rejecting the contrary-to-fact conditional hypothesis, Powell responded to the minority opinion justices who upheld it as follows:

> I disagree with much that is said in their opinion. They would require as a justification for a program . . . only two findings: (i) that there has been some form of discrimination against the preferred minority groups "by society at large" . . . and (ii) that "there is reason to believe" that the disparate impact sought to be rectified by the program is the "product" of such discrimination.
>
> The breadth of this hypothesis is unprecedented in our constitutional system. The first step is easily taken. . . . The second step, however, involves a speculative leap: but for this discrimination by society at large, Bakke "would have failed to qualify for admission" because Negro applicants . . . would have made better scores. *Not one word in the record supports this conclusion.* [italics added] . . . [it] offers no standards for courts to use in applying such a presumption of causation to other racial or ethnic classifications. . . .
>
> There is no principled basis for deciding which groups would merit 'heightened judicial solicitude' and which would not . . . . This kind of variable sociological and political analysis necessary to produce such rankings simply does not lie within the judicial competence. . . . isolated segments of our vast governmental structures are not competent to make those decisions at least in the absence of legislative mandates and legislatively determined criteria.[11]

The final and most important case to substantiate the claim that affirmative action in any interesting sense is illegal is *Adarand Constructors, Inc. v. Pena* (1995). Congress had, in the Minority Business Enterprise provision of the Public Works Employment Act of 1977, required that 10 percent of the federal funds allocated to state and local governments for public works projects must be used to purchase goods and services from minority-owned businesses even if nonminority-owned firms offered a lower bid. The reasoning behind this legislation was that minorities had been discriminated against in the past and were due redress. This is a case of punitive action (definition 2). Some had suggested that it constituted legislative endorsement of either compensation (definition 4) or preference (definition 5).

The Adarand decision effectively reduced this policy to the punitive version (definition 2). One reason this decision is so important is that it clarified a somewhat bewildering series of previous decisions.[12]

As Justice O'Connor expressed it in *Adarand*:

> The Court's failure to produce a majority opinion in Bakke, Fullilove, and Wygant left unresolved the proper analysis for remedial race-based governmental action. See *United States v. Paradise*, 480 U.S., at 166 [43 FEP Cases, at 7] (plurality opinion of Brennan, J.) ('[A]lthough this court has consistently held that some elevated level of scrutiny is required when a racial or ethnic distinction is made for remedial purposes, it has yet to reach consensus on the appropriate constitutional analysis'); *Sheet Metal Workers v. EEOC*, 478 U.S. 421, 480 [41 FEP Cases 107, 130] (1986) (plurality opinion of Brennan, J.). Lower courts found this lack of guidance unsettling. See, e.g., *Kromnick v. School District of Philadelphia*, 739 F.2d 894, 901 [35 FEP Cases 538, 544] (CA3 1984) ('The absence of an Opinion of the Court in either Bakke or Fullilove and the concomitant failure of the Court to articulate an analytic framework supporting the judgments makes the position of the lower federal courts considering the constitutionality of affirmative action programs somewhat vulnerable'). . . . The Court resolved the issue, at least in part, in 1989. . . . A majority of the court in *Croson* held that 'the standard of review under the Equal Protection Clause is not dependent on the race of those burdened or benefitted by a particular classification,' and that the single standard of review for racial classifications should be 'strict scrutiny.'

"Strict scrutiny" means that previous discrimination must be established, that is, we are dealing with definition 2, and that the redress must be carefully limited in time and place.

Justice O'Connor continues:

> Accordingly, we hold today that all racial classifications, imposed by whatever federal, state, or local government actor, must be analyzed by a reviewing court under strict scrutiny. In other words, such classifications are constitutional only if they are narrowly tailored measures that further compelling governmental interests.
>
> Our action today makes explicit what Justice Powell thought implicit in the Fullilove lead opinion: federal racial classifications, like those of a State, must serve a compelling governmental interest, and must be narrowly tailored to further that interest.[13]

Affirmative action as either compensation or preference is illegal. If such policies are so pervasive, this reflects the illegal and unauthorized activities of government bureaucracies (a widespread problem that goes way beyond affirmative action); it reflects those activist judges who confuse the judicial process with the legislative process and who confuse their own values with the true moral foundations of the United States; it reflects the ideological agenda of many academics; it reflects the unscrupulous activities of politicians whose careers are predicated on maintaining voting blocks based upon racial clientage; and it reflects fear in the business community of endless litigation.

Affirmative Action Is Immoral

As a society the United States is committed to six major normative premises:

1. We are committed to the belief in a *cosmic order* ("In God We Trust").
2. We are committed to the belief in the sanctity of the *individual*.

The *Declaration of Independence* declares:

> We hold these truths to be self-evident, that all men are created equal, that they are endowed by their Creator with certain unalienable Rights, that among these are Life, Liberty, and the pursuit of Happiness. That to secure these rights, Governments are instituted among Men, deriving their just powers from the consent of the governed.

In his dissent in the *Plessy v. Ferguson* case (1896), Justice Harlan enunciated the fundamental principle of individuality in a specific way, namely that the U.S. Constitution is and ought to be *color-blind*.[14] This reiterates the point that it is the individual as such and not membership in a group that defines who we are. "Our constitution is color-blind, and neither knows nor tolerates classes among citizens. . . . The law regards man as man, and takes no account of his surroundings or of his color."[15]

In arguing against the then majority view, Harlan warned that the separate but equal doctrine "will, in time prove to be quite as pernicious as the decision made by this tribunal in the Dred Scott case."[16] The point of Harlan's observation is that invidious comparisons or classifications deny individuals the equal protection of the laws. Finally, Harlan reiterated that "the destinies of the two races, in this country, are indissolubly linked together, and the interests of both require that the common government of all shall not permit the seeds of race hate to be planted under the sanction of law."[17]

In his famous "I have a dream" speech on the steps of the Lincoln Memorial in 1964, Dr. Martin Luther King, Jr., looked forward to when his children would "live in a nation where they will not be judged by the color of their skin but by the content of their character."

Harlan's view has also been echoed in a recent statement by Justice Scalia:

> government can never have a "compelling interest" in discriminating on the basis of race in order to 'make up' for past racial discrimination in the opposite direction. . . . Individuals who have been wronged by unlawful racial discrimination should be made whole; but under our constitution there can be no such thing as either a creditor or debtor race. That concept is alien to the constitution's focus upon the individual. . . . To pursue the concept of racial entitlement—even for the most admirable and benign of purposes—is to reinforce and preserve for future mischief the way of thinking that produced race slavery, race privilege, and race hatred. In the eyes of government, we are just one race here. It is American.[18]

The sanctity of the individual has to be understood in a special moral way.

The Sanctity of the individual means:

a. that human beings possess the rational capacity to recognize a universal cosmic order;
b. that human beings have the internal capacity to be unconstrained in their decision to act in accordance with the cosmic order, that is, *free will*;
c. that true freedom and dignity consist in the inner or self-discipline that comes with the exercise of these capacities; and
d. that these capacities can only be discovered retrospectively by their exercise; limited government and a free market economy are the only political and economic institutions compatible with individual dignity; the justification of such institutions is not their efficiency but their efficacy for the exercise of personal autonomy.

The continuous Western meaning of freedom is self-government; the modern version of freedom is the self-government of the individual (not the classical notion of a self-governing polis).

This special moral understanding of individuality has most recently been enunciated by Justice Clarence Thomas in his condemnation of affirmative action (understood in the preferential sense).

> I believe that there is a moral [and] constitutional equivalence . . . between laws designed to subjugate a race and those that distribute benefits on the basis of race in order to foster some current notion of equality. Government cannot make us equal; it can only recognize, respect, and protect us as equal before the law. That these programs may have been motivated, in part, by good intentions cannot provide refuge from the principles that under our Constitution, the government may not make distinctions on the basis of race. As far as the Constitution is concerned, it is irrelevant whether a government's racial classifications are drawn by those who wish to oppress a race or by those who have a sincere desire to help those thought to be disadvantaged. There can be no doubt that the paternalism that appears to lie at the heart of this program is at war with the principle of inherent equality that underlies and infuses our Constitution. . . . These programs not only raise grave constitutional questions, they also undermine the moral basis of the equal protection principle. Purchased at the price of immeasurable human suffering, the equal protection principle reflects our Nation's under-standing that such classifications ultimately have a destructive impact on the individual and our society . . . there can be no doubt that racial paternalism and its unintended consequences can be as poisonous and pernicious as any other form of discrimination.[19]

3. We are committed to the belief that the communal good is not something over and above the good of the individuals who make up the community.
4. We are committed to the belief that the *rule of law* means due process and equality before the law (i.e., equality of opportunity and not equality of result).

The popular understanding of these principles is reflected in a poll conducted by *USA Today* (24 March, 1995, 3A). In this survey, 73 percent favor "special efforts to find qualified minorities and women and then encouraging them to apply for jobs with that company," and at the same time 84 percent of the public oppose "favoring a minority who is less qualified than a white applicant, when filling a job in a business that has few minority workers."

5. We subscribe to a *republican* or limited form of government and not a democracy. It is a system in which liberty is established by restraining government through checks and balances of power.

6. We embrace a *free market economy*. The only real good is the good of the individual. Free market economies are especially important because they combine efficiency and morality.

The wealth created in a free market economy is a good thing because: (a) It enhances the human condition. Income is not merely a means to consumer satisfaction, nor merely an incentive. Rather, income is *a means to accomplishment*. (b) Wealth liberates us from the culture of poverty. Whereas in the medieval world it was wealth that created a scandal, the scandal of the modern world is the existence of poverty. (c) Private wealth provides a check on the power of the government, and leads to the expansion of individual liberties. (d) Finally, wealth provides the dynamic of social reform.

Every one of these points is invoked in one of President Abraham Lincoln's speeches:

I beg you to remember this, not merely for my sake, but for yours. I happen, temporarily, to occupy the White House. I am a living witness that any one of your children may look to come here as my father's child has. It is in order that each one of you may have, through this free government which we have enjoyed, an open field and a fair chance for your industry, enterprise, and intelligence; that you may all have equal privileges in the race of life, with all its desirable human aspirations. It is for this the struggle should be maintained. . . . The nation is worth fighting for, to secure such an inestimable jewel.[20]

Most of the participants in the affirmative action debate subscribe to these fundamental moral principles. Even those who have actively supported the implementation of preferential programs agree that these are the fundamental principles. What they have urged is that the programs of preference are a temporary means to achieve the fundamental values. Joseph Califano, former Secretary of Health, Education, and Welfare under President Carter, wrote in 1989 that affirmative action was intended "only as a temporary expedient to speed blacks' entry into the social and economic mainstream. . . . it was never conceived as a permanent program and its time is running out."[21] Even in his dissent in *Bakke*, Justice Blackmun stated that "in order to get beyond racism, we must first take account of race," thereby acknowledging that affirmative action at best is a temporary expedient. What is at issue is whether we can temporarily suspend these principles for a desirable end, that is, whether the end justifies the means. This is an issue we take up in the next section.

One last thing we want to note about our fundamental moral principles is their logical status. In calling these our fundamental norms, we are not describing how people actually behave but how they ought to behave. Having these as norms permits us to identify those cases where we have failed to live up to them. Too many proponents of affirmative action fail to understand the logical status of norms, thinking that they have either invalidated the norms (e.g., color-blindness) or they have invalidated our claim to have identified the norm as norm because of our failure to live up to it. In practice, the United States has failed in part and continues to fail to live up to the ideal of a color-blind society—but these are grounds for trying harder, not for adopting race consciousness as a norm.

There are two moral arguments routinely presented in favor of affirmative action. One reflects definition 4 (compensation) and one reflects definition 5 (preference). We turn now to those arguments and my rebuttal of them.

The compensation argument maintains that slavery and discrimination practiced over a long period of time have disadvantaged the present generations of African Americans so that they (1) cannot compete effectively, and (2) therefore, should be awarded positions and promotions in a manner consistent with the punitive principles as enunciated in definition 2. This is not a strictly legal argument because the law demands that overt and provable practices of discrimination against specific individuals must be the basis of redress and remediation.

The argument makes two assumptions. The first is the statistical assumption that every group possesses the same talents and interests in the same proportion as their percentage in the population. The second assumption is that it is possible to construct a contrary-to-fact conditional argument of an historical-causal kind to substantiate this claim of what might have been.

The compensation argument can be rebutted on the following grounds:

(1) It misconstrues the legal nature of compensation.[22] In order for "compensation" to be invoked, we must (a) show that the injury—in this case failure to achieve—was caused by discrimination (or analogous phenomenon), (b) identify the party at fault, and (c) calculate a relevant benefit to be paid by the party at fault. Item (a)

is never established in a direct causal fashion; with regard to item (b) the perpetrating parties are either long dead or identified in a hopelessly amorphous fashion as "society at large"; with regard to item (c), there is no way to extract a benefit given what we have said about item (b), and any relevant benefit would be monetary, not a position that the alleged injured party is unable to hold if injured.

(2) The punitive redress that the courts have imposed never involve giving positions to people who cannot compete effectively but to people who can compete but were never given the opportunity to compete.

(3) There is absolutely no evidence for the extraordinary statistical assumption; moreover, if you believe that some groups are under-represented then it follows as a matter of logical truth that some groups are overrepresented. Who is willing to point the finger at allegedly overrepresented groups?

(4) To put such a policy into action leads to *reverse discrimination*, that is, penalizing innocent individuals by denying them opportunities; this amounts to believing that the end justifies the means.

(5) There is no way to substantiate the contrary-to-fact conditional argument (Justice Powell's point in *Bakke*): (a) That a significant number of African Americans fully participate is counterevidence— Why were they, unlike their brethren, not harmed to the point of being unable to compete effectively? (b) We can construct equally plausible (or implausible) contrary-to-fact scenarios, for example, the African American descendants of slaves are beneficiaries of slavery in that they have better lives (or even are alive in greater numbers) than they would have been if slavery had not existed. (c) We can reverse the reverse-discrimination with the following equally plausible (or implausible) scenario—African Americans actually owe compensation to the United States! The failure of present generations of African Americans to participate fully is not the result of slavery and discrimination but of other factors, for some of which they bear responsibility (a point to be expanded upon later). Moreover, this failure to participate fully has actually harmed non-African Americans more than helped them because it has wasted enormous resources and thereby limited the number of opportunities available to everybody else.

I think this last scenario deserves to some extent to be considered seriously. Many who argue for affirmative action see the economy as a zero-sum game with a constant pie, so that in order to gain a bigger slice of pie one has to take a piece from someone else. This is a fundamental misperception of both economics and of the fundamental values of the United States. They misunderstand—hence, they have the wrong diagnosis of the problems at issue.

The incorrect diagnosis (based on faulty economics) is that Whites have taken too much of something and thereby denied access to it by African Americans.[23] The correct diagnosis, I suggest, is that by failing to embody certain values, African Americans have deprived themselves of opportunities. Because they have the wrong diagnosis, they propose the wrong (and counterproductive) remedies such as affirmative action, which is a form of redistribution. A useful analogy is to recall that in the 1950's it was fashionable for intellectuals in Latin America to diagnose their economic underdevelopment as a consequence of capitalist exploitation, specifically the notion that Latin America and the Third World in general were condemned to be providers of raw materials. The recent explosive growth of their economies coincided with the acceptance of a new diagnosis that Latin America had not been capitalist enough.

Let us now turn to the preference argument. This argument maintains that because of the history of slavery and discrimination, African Americans have never been made to feel that they belong. This is especially problematic in a democratic society. Affirmative action is a way to help African Americans realize the basic values of the United States.

This argument rests upon a number of misconceptions. First of all, it is conceptualizing the problem in terms of the notion of a "democratic society." This is incorrect for two reasons. The United States is not a democracy but a republic. In a republic, government is limited to serving other interests because those interests reflect the basic rights of individuals. That is, political institutions are subordinate to moral preconceptions. James Madison argued that it was a utopian delusion to expect unanimity; factions were inevitable; the instrument for avoiding factional strife was checks and balances. Democracy is not an intrinsic end but a quite limited institutional arrangement that reflects more fundamental values. There is a serious confusion here of normative priority. Politicizing U.S. society and politicizing the issue of why African Americans do not participate as much as we would all wish is the wrong way to approach this issue.

Second, conceptualizing the problem from the point of view of groups (that is, African Americans conceived of as a voting block) is symptomatic of the failure to develop a sense of individuality. The question is not whether my group participates fully, the question is whether "I" or "you" participate fully.

Third, part of the reason that so many African Americans feel that they do not belong is that they have failed to embrace, much less understand, the fundamental values that animate our society.

Affirmative Action Is Impractical and Illogical

So far I have argued that affirmative action is both illegal and immoral. Now I want to show what happens when we try to put this policy into action.

There are three sometimes overlapping versions of the actual policy applications of affirmative action. Sometimes, the policy is meant to reflect the compensation version; sometimes the policy reflects the preference version understood as a form of compensation; sometimes the policy reflects pure preference without any pretense of compensation. I will identify these as I go along.

Numbers Game

One of the reasons why affirmative action as compensation and prefer-ence are promoted is the belief that widespread discrimination is an obstacle to full participation. It turns out that the existence of discrimina-tion is much less wide spread than previously believed; at least it is difficult to establish legally. Moreover, all the overt forms of discrimination have been outlawed. Still, it seems to be the case that many African Americans do not participate fully. So committed to the diagnosis of discrimination are the supporters of affirmative action that they even persist in labeling as "racist" rebuttals of their arguments or the annoyance of those who do not like to see the ideals of American society trashed.

Rather than surrender the diagnosis, advocates of affirmative action maintained that discrimination was much more "subtle." How do they know that there is subtle discrimination? They claim to know this because they assume that in a truly nondiscriminatory society, the percentage of African Americans in desirable and competitive positions would reflect their percentage in the population as a whole (adjusted for age). Hence, affirmative action as a policy must include an "effects" test because "intent" is hard to establish. As a result, quotas, goals, timetables, and so on, must be instituted.

> Vague outreach efforts will also be insufficient in situations where hiring procedures—whatever they are—can be manipulated by prejudicial personnel officers. Lack of specificity invites evasion. Moreover, even impartial employers find unspecified outreach requirements difficult to administer. Without definite numerical targets, they have no standard of reasonable progress in the recruitment of minorities.[24]

There are three things wrong with this policy argument. First, it is an example of *ad hoc* emendation of a hypothesis. Failing to find evidence to support their case, they resort to speculative hypotheses to shore up their failed case. Postulating more and more subtle forms of alleged racism is just like adding an extra epicycle—it does nothing to help the argument and calls for a major reexamination of basic assumptions. Second, the numerical assumption is, as we have already argued, totally without evidential support. Thomas Sowell has called this the "noble lie of our time."[25] Third, it is an example of the fallacy of invincible ignorance, that is, the refusal to accept any other diagnosis of the problem. Even if it were the case that native ability and interest was present in some relevant statistical sense this still would not establish that discrimination was the cause of the lack of full participation.

The last point can be made in another important way. African Americans fail to qualify for admission to many highly competitive programs such as medical school because of the failure to achieve high enough scores on examinations. In this sense there is no illegal discrimination. However, advocates of affirmative action claim that failure to gain a high score reflects the lingering effects of past discrimination.

To begin with, there is no evidence of the lingering effects of discrimination except the failure to gain a high score. To claim otherwise is once again to appeal to the contrary-to-fact conditional argument that Justice Powell claimed to be totally lacking in evidential support. This amounts to advocates of affirmative action presenting a circular argument. Failure to achieve is the result of the lingering effects of slavery and Jim Crow, and the evidence of this is the failure to achieve.

What makes this argument even worse is the following: If failure is the result of the lingering effects of past discrimination, then how are we to choose which African Americans get preferential treatment? The answer given by supporters of affirmative action is that we rank order African Americans and choose those who score highest in their own racial group. The trouble with this reply is that if low scores are evidence of the lingering effects of discrimination then those with the lowest scores might be the one's most discriminated against. Perhaps we should then choose those from the bottom of the African American list. When it suits their convenience we play by the rules of merit; when it suits their convenience we play by the rules of alleged victimization. This is just one of the examples of the illogical policy implications of accepting the diagnosis offered by partisans of affirmative action.

The numbers game argument was intended to justify compensation and to frame preference policies and to do so on the assumptions that (1) African Americans have clearly demonstrated talents, and either (2) the talents have been denied outlets, or (3) the talents had not been allowed to develop because of past discrimination (lingering-effects hypothesis).

No one challenges assumption (2). It turns out, however, that (1) is the least plausible assumption. Where African Americans have been granted access to competitive positions (medical school, law school, etc.) under affirmative action conditions they have not, as a group, demonstrated excellence. The appeal to (3) in some version is intended as an explanation for this.

This lingering-effects hypothesis has already been challenged in two ways. First, there is no way to prove it. Second, there are many other explanations for why people might not achieve their potential or fully participate. Rather than stay locked in to an analysis predicated on conditions that no longer exist (i.e., slavery, Jim Crow), and rather than harping on discrimination, why not propose affirmative action as preference in terms of where we want U.S. society to be?

This is exactly what is done with the following four arguments, which advocate preference without any necessary appeal to compensation.

Role Models

According to the role model argument, African Americans should be placed in prominent roles in order to raise the aspirations of other African

Americans and thereby let them see that they too can be accepted and encourage them to become fully participatory. This argument need not be accompanied by any reference to discrimination and it need not make any assumptions about how talent is statistically distributed.

There are four obvious objections to this policy. First, it is illegal and immoral. Second, the policy is counterproductive, for what it reinforces is the perception that African Americans can only succeed if held to lower or different standards. Third, if African Americans "need" role models then what this shows is that too many of them are still thinking in terms of their group membership and have not developed the requisite sense of individual autonomy. Finally, the policy is based on false assumptions, for the first successful African Americans and many current successful African Americans did not have role models of the same race.

Multicultural Society

According to the multicultural argument, the United States is a multi-cultural society in which people from different backgrounds must learn to live and work together. One obstacle to positive interaction is the presence of stereotypes (even in ethnic humor) about members of other groups. Black stereotypes are the result of a lack of interaction and the dearth of African Americans in prominent positions. Affirmative action in the form of preference is just one of many policies designed to overcome these stereotypes.

There are five objections to this policy. The first three are the same objections mentioned above with regard to role models. More important, I contest the diagnosis of stereotypes. I do not believe that the overwhelm-ing majority of Americans are either hostile to or unable to get along with African Americans because of racial stereotyping. To begin with, some of the things that go under the category of stereotyping are not stereotyping. It is an unfortunate fact that one-third of all African American teenage males will be involved negatively with the justice system; that is ten times the percentage for White teenage males. Feeling threatened by the presence of such teenagers is not a matter of either prejudice or of stereotyping but a justifiable prudential reaction. What most Americans (and many foreign visitors) object to is the perceived failure of so many African Americans to embody fundamental values such as responsibility and civility. Of course, there are very notable exceptions, but in dealing with strangers we have no recourse but to rely upon what common sense tells us. Bringing people together who do not share the same values actually exacerbates conflict and leads to the notorious "white flight." Finally, in a social atmosphere that penalizes and castigates those who dare to mention this objection, we get not only more withdrawal or flight but also start to build hidden resentments. What proponents of affirmative action have done is offend the moral sensibilities and assassinate the character of their detractors and at the same time claim that the negative feelings they have provoked is a cause of or justification for their provocation! In short, they have created a new social problem.

I note in passing that Multiculturalism is sometimes tied to democracy. It is claimed that since the majority of Americans will someday not be descended from northern Europeans or even Europeans, then numerical balancing and preference should be instituted to reflect that reality. I have already objected to the appeal to democracy as inconsistent with our fundamental values. I add to that objection the following observation. The issue is not what color America is but what values Americans share. Our culture is not defined by its origins or one particular practice such as democracy, rather it is defined by multiple characteristics, such as the importance of individuality, the rule of law, and a republican form of government.

New Perspectives

Another argument offered for affirmative action purely as a form of preference is that African Americans bring new perspectives to bear on traditional ways of doing and thinking about things. However, there are three objections and one interesting problem raised by this policy. The first objection is that it conflicts with the very idea of permitting African Americans to join the mainstream by maintaining that there is more than one stream. The idea that African Americans need to be cultivated in a unique context could lead us back to the system that the U.S. Supreme Court rejected in *Brown v. Board of Education* (1954).[26]

This often turns out to be a variation of the democracy argument, namely, that since African Americans are 12 percent of the population, then 12 percent of everything (positions, programs, policies) somehow should be defined by them. I have already indicated that this is based on a misperception of the role of democracy within a liberal culture such as ours.

The second objection is that the so-called new perspectives often means institutionalizing a certain hypothesis about why African Americans fail to participate fully. That is, the way in which African Americans would now participate is not by doing what other people do but by serving as facilitators who reiterate constantly in consciousness raising sessions the hypothesis that the failure to participate fully is the result of the "lingering effects of slavery and discrimination." This has as its consequences the legitimation of a specific diagnosis and a policy of remediation without serious discussion. So what justifies the policy is a specific diagnosis and the whole point of the policy is to delegitimate alternative diagnoses. Such a policy politicizes institutional practices, that is, it undermines more fundamental values.

The third objection is that this emphasis on new perspectives and multiculturalism conflicts with the claim that African Americans are just as talented as everyone else and have been denied opportunities to display their ability. The multicultural claim is that African Americans are different and cannot be held to the same standards as everyone else. There is a disturbing undertone of racism in the implication that African Americans are unable to compete with others so we must find something that only they can do. The concept of a peculiarly African American perspective that cannot be shared with others or modified by interaction with others betrays the existence of a pervasive insecurity that seeks to immunize itself from criticism.

The really interesting question raised by this policy is whether the new perspectives are consistent with the fundamental values of the United States. If so, then the new perspectives are important clarifications of fundamental values. If the values belong to all of us, then the exploration and espousal of those perspectives become common property open to all. This cannot be used to limit access to employment positions anymore than one can argue that only Italians ought to be permitted to sing Puccini.

Preventing Antisocial Behavior

The argument regarding behavior assumes that "overrepresentation" in antisocial behavior (committing crimes, drug use, etc.) is the result of "underrepresentation" in prominent positions or that the policy of prefer-ence designed to overcome 'underrepresentation' will lead to African Americans being less likely to engage in antisocial behavior. One variation of this argument of affirmative action as a preferential policy is the so-called need to break psychological barriers. I have already had occasion to disagree with this in my discussion of role models. Finally, no one has ever presented any evidence that eliminating "underrepresentation" eliminates "overrepresentation".

A second variation is based upon the assumption that African Ameri-cans engage in antisocial behavior because their ambitions are thwarted. This variation is mistaken in part because it fails to take into account that the majority of African Americans do not engage in antisocial behavior. This variation also assumes that antisocial behavior is solely the result of the failure of the larger social context to provide opportunities. Once more we see an emerging paradigm that attempts to explain human action in terms that ignore the moral dimension to human autonomy. I shall have more to say about this below.

A third variation presupposes that African Americans are inherently inferior and that unless all of us subscribe to some official mythology about equality, we shall have serious social conflict. Affirmative action as preference is, then, part of a publicly sanctioned myth. This variation, besides being condescending is also a form of extortion. More important, it keeps assuming that full participation is identical to symbolic and highly visible social prominence. This strikes me as misunderstanding the fundamental problems that confront African Americans, but for the moment, I shall have to postpone discussion of this issue.

The Failure of Social Engineering

There is one final objection. This involves the idea that affirmative action as a policy, either of compensation or preference, is a form of social engineering. By *social engineering* I mean the following: (1) the conceptualization of the human predicament as a series of problems to be solved; (2) the belief that there is a form of social technology comparable to the technology we use to manipulate and reconstruct the physical environment (e.g., build a bridge, replace a hip); (3) the assumption that this social technology is based upon social scientific information about human nature that is equivalent in cognitive status to physical scientific information; and (4) the assumption that the government in some form is to be the institution that commands the resources and wields the power that permits it to direct the social reconstruction.

The routine operation of the legal system is not an example of social engineering. Punitive forms of "affirmative action" (definition 2) are not examples of social engineering since they do not seek to reconstruct society according to some plan or according to some assumed scientific truths about human nature; rather, they redress violations of the law. Routine operations of the executive bureaucracy, such as enforcing pollution controls or fixing interest rates, are not examples of social engineering; rather, they provide the framework within which other individuals and institutions conduct their lives.

However, socialism, understood as the attempted centralized (governmental) planning and control of the economy (i.e., definition of objectives, allocation of resources) is an example of social engineering. Socialism is the attempt to control the production, distribution (and sometimes consumption) of economic resources. It is today generally accepted that socialism is a failure.

The classic argument against social engineering in the economic realm was advanced by F. Hayek.[27] According to Hayek, it is impossible for any individual or organization to possess the information necessary to carry out economic planning on the social scale. This is not a mere technical limitation. Not possessing the requisite information means that the social/economic world is not a mechanical system where sufficient information about inputs determines outputs. The social world is a dynamic system (organic and historical) where action or policy is based upon some conceptualization of the world within which we are acting and where any action or policy might sufficiently change that world so that some adjustment must be made in the conceptualization. Since every policy changes the reality, there is no way to have a policy that does not require constant readjustment.

Policy, whether individual or institutional, is based upon norms. In order for social planning to have any meaning there must be a social whole of norms that subsumes the goals of the individuals who make up the society. The United States (and the West in general), as I have asserted above, denies the existence of a social or common good that subsumes the good of the individuals who compose it. For us, the social good is no more than the good of the individuals who compose our society. As a result, social planning can only be misconceived or be a mask for a private agenda. The political process in the United States is designed to negotiate and mediate the evolving interests of individuals, groups, and institutions within the framework of the Constitution. All such negotiation begins from the status quo and proceeds by due process; it does not begin with or claim to move toward some utopian resolution. In short, social engineering misconceives the moral and political process by construing it as a technical process.

Let us see how affirmative action as either compensation or preference exemplifies the failure of social engineering. The advocates of affirmative action in these senses presume that there is an ideal social whole in which each designated group enjoys a percentage of resources (e.g., employment positions) equal to their percentage in the population. The curious thing about this presumption is that no group in the United States, including the ones designated by advocates of affirmative action, actually believes this. Even within the African American group, a majority (however slim) does not presume that there is such an ideal social whole. Only self-designated elites (e.g., politicians such as Jesse Jackson or academics such as Leonard Jeffries) among African Americans make this claim. This claim, I conclude, reflects either a colossal misconception on the part of these elites, or the claim is a mask for the self-promotion of these elites.

Second, affirmative action (hereafter I mean it only in the sense of compensation or preference) as a policy presumes that the promotion of the elite will (through role modeling) end "overrepresentation" in prisons and welfare. We have challenged this presumption as totally lacking in credibility. So, not only does affirmative action represent a bogus goal, it will ultimately fail to achieve a goal on which there is consensus, namely, fuller participation of African Americans.

Third, affirmative action presumes a kind of crude economic determinism. By this I mean that it presumes that changes in economic condition, such as the control of scarce resources and desirable employment positions, determines changes throughout the rest of the social structure. There is no serious argument for this presumption. Moreover, it is clear that if there is some relation between economic conditions and general cultural conditions the relationship is mutual, so that changes in personal values influence one's capacity to gain resources.

Fourth, social engineering is far more invasive than is usually realized.

If discrimination (racism, lingering effects) is as pervasive throughout our culture as advocates of affirmative action claim, then it will not be sufficient to reallocate jobs. Everything in the culture will be subject to reallocation from housing to spouses.[28]

Fifth, it is impossible for public agencies to formulate rules of eligibility for any social program that will not irrationally exclude some of the very people for whom the program is intended and include people for whom the program was not intended. This does not reflect incompetence on the part of bureaucrats, rather it is a reflection of the logic of rule formulation. For example, the program of Aid to Families with Dependent Children is designed to help families with dependent children to get out of the poverty trap. It operates by establishing a maximum income beyond which it will not provide aid. This policy is both underinclusive and overinclusive. It is underinclusive because there is a group of working poor with dependent children who earn slightly above the maximum; it is overinclusive because the arbitrary cut-off point encourages some of the working poor to give up their jobs in order to earn benefits they lose by working.

The only way to avoid this problem is to leave it to individual discretion to decide who is really in need of preference or compensation. Such discretion is possible in a private charity but is impractical in a public agency where objective criteria must be used in order to avoid charges of corruption or incompetence. So something seemingly "objective" like race (sex, surname) becomes the definition of eligibility. Many other individuals who do not meet these narrow criteria but are precisely among the people the social program is intended to help will fail to qualify for eligibility. At the same time, many extremely privileged and elite members of society, including upper-middle-class African Americans, suddenly become beneficiaries of a program really intended to help others.

In a hybrid society such as America, how does one classify a person? Suppose a child to have an African American father and an Asian American mother. What is the child? Does the child get plus points for the first and minus points for the second (because Asian Americans are so successful)? Being an African American and being female are supposed to be detrimental, but African American females participate more fully than African American males—so how do we calculate the "deservedness" in this case?

Sixth, as soon as a program rewards those who claim to be victimized, it increases the number of individuals and groups who claim to be victims. For example, we can imagine individuals beginning to wonder at how much "psychic damage" is experienced by left-handed people in a right-handed world. Only now are statistics being collected to show the differential impact on the lives of left-handed people. Is there any limit on who may claim to be a victim?

Market Solutions

The case I have been building so far against affirmative action is a case against compensation and preference. I wish to go even further and suggest that discrimination should be illegal only if practiced by government. That is, some of the same reasons that make social engineering impractical and counterproductive suggest that there should be no law against private discrimination, only laws against discrimination by government.

The distinction, as William Allen has argued, is an important one.[29] To outlaw discrimination in general is to make the government the arbiter both of how discrimination is to be identified and defined and also of how it is to be overcome. It is to give to the government the power to discriminate in the name of overcoming discrimination; and in practice it leads to state-sponsored discrimination.

This suggestion will strike many as shocking, especially (but not only) in light of the unacceptable treatment of African Americans in the South prior to the advent of the Civil Rights Movement. However, it is important to note that it was precisely discrimination by state government that marked the condition of the South. Federal action was justified precisely because it was needed to overcome state-sponsored discrimination, in this case sponsored by state governments.

Would such a policy of outlawing only government discrimination lead to the widespread return of private discrimination? The logic of a free market system suggests otherwise. A qualified version of this proposal, suggested by Tibor Machan, is that private individuals and organizations be allowed to discriminate but only if that is their publicly announced policy.[30] They could be sued only if they practiced discrimination but failed to announce it publicly in advance. Under this proposal, private universities, that is, those who do not accept government funding, would be allowed to inaugurate "affirmative action" programs. The presumption behind this suggestion is that between general public revulsion and the workings of the market, private discriminators would not be able to compete. The economy of the South began to boom only and precisely when companies could operate there under market conditions and without state-sanctioned discrimination.

Another point worth noting is that if there are valuable alternative ways of doing and conceptualizing things, as multiculturalists often argue, then it is much more likely that they will be discovered in the market place than by bureaucratic decree.[31]

Affirmative Action Undermines American Society

The ideal of America is that of a community of free and responsible individuals. Affirmative action supplants that with the concept of group membership and group entitlement. This leads in time to the balkanization of society. I said earlier that affirmative action is an issue almost exclusively for African Americans. From its inception in the 1964 Civil Rights Act, affirmative action was seen as a form of clientage tying African Americans to the Democratic party. But it has now taken on a life of its own.

This is seen in the gerrymandering of African American voting districts. It is behind Lani Guinier's call for the permanent institutionalization of African American representatives.[32] It is in Louis Farrakan's agenda.

> In favoring racial separatism, the Nation of Islam has taken ideas long favored by the liberal establishment—separately tracked school admissions, racial employment criteria, segregated campus dormitories and congressional districts—to their illogical conclusion. . . . Both the uplifting and ugly sides of Farrakan's movement flow from an ideology that posits blacks as aliens, as members of a proud and separate polity. Farrakan does not think that blacks should wear America's uniform or be subject to America's laws, or that non-blacks should own property or run businesses in black neighborhoods. The only antidote to this message is the cultivation of an overarching sense of American identity.[33]

Balkanization undermines an American ideal; and its practice elsewhere in the world, as Thomas Sowell reminds us, has been a disaster.

Where separate group identities are government-subsidized—often under the general label of 'multiculturalism' in Australia, Britain, Canada, and the United States—an artificial Balkanization is fostered, with utter disregard of the tragic historic consequences of Balkanization in many parts of Asia and Africa, as well as in the Balkans themselves.[34]

One of the negative consequences of the policy is that it will encourage others to pursue balkanization.

Affirmative action undermines the fragile confidence of African Americans who are struggling to participate fully. You cannot be an autonomous individual if you must always worry whether your position is truly earned and deserved or whether it reflects condescension on the part of others.[35] Often, African Americans seek to shore up fragile egos either with the false consciousness that everyone else is against them or by cynical denials that merit is ever an issue. One does not have to be blind to the injustices of the world in order to recognize the false consciousness that affirmative action engenders.

Affirmative action exacerbates group conflict. When affirmative action was first instituted in the early 1970s it was largely confined to education (where it was welcomed with open arms), to government, and to businesses that operated as publicly endorsed monopolies, such as utility companies. The public, by and large, had no direct contact with or interest in it. However, after two decades of expansion, and in the presence of an economy where middle-management positions are becoming less numerous, affirmative action has become a pervasive feature of professional life. In the eyes of many people, affirmative action is just another injustice wherein some people obtain privileges based on race.

Affirmative action undermines the integrity of institutions in which it is practiced. Higher education is an example in point. Part, but only part, of the origin of grade inflation had been the vast expansion of the pool of unqualified and ill-prepared high school graduates. Loathe to flunk out students for fear of economic and political reprisals, university educators have had to inflate grades. Grade-inflation leads to a "dumbing-down" of content. The end result is that most universities are no longer institutions of higher education.

Black studies is another example. No doubt there is something interesting and worth studying about everything; no doubt, there are Black studies programs that maintain standards; but there is something else that is not in doubt. In order to hire African American applicants who would not otherwise qualify for positions as faculty, special programs are created—programs where the overwhelming majority of applicants are likely to be African Americans. Then, in order to ensure that African American faculty will have students to teach, special requirements are introduced into the curriculum requiring that all students take these courses. Forced to justify these requirements as opposed to others, university administrators and sympathetic faculty engage in an attack on traditional values that have served to prioritize requirements in the past. Arguments against the traditional priorities range all the way from extreme cultural relativism to official endorsement of the historical and sociological assumptions on which affirmative action is based. Rather than being just another hypothesis up for argument, claims about "underrepresentation" are elevated into articles of faith. Who better to teach these articles of faith than African Americans? In a culture of condescension, how many faculty and students will openly decry the now hallowed hypothesis?

Speech codes are the final effect of affirmative action. None of us wants to endorse bad manners or slander, but what counts as slander has been redefined to reflect acceptance and rejection of certain analyses of public policy issues. Those who question the favored hypothesis are excoriated. For example, to deny that racism is responsible for all the problems faced by African Americans is to be accused of insensitivity. When students understandably respond intemperately they are accused of racism and held accountable for violations of the speech code.

Instead of claiming to censor opinions, it is always suggested that we censor inappropriate expressions of opinions. But John Stuart Mill pointed something out about this long ago. There is no formal way to do this without ultimately silencing certain kinds of dissent. It is better to recognize that people who express themselves in a morally inexcusable fashion invariably hurt themselves and their cause. Speech codes and the arguments for them are "open sesame's" to inhibit anything of which we disapprove, and such codes invariably create the impression that since critics cannot be answered logically they are responded to with coercion.

The response to the foregoing argument, given by those who support speech codes, is that African American students are unusually sensitive and that part of the reason for their lack of academic success is the hostile feelings around them, especially hostile forms of speech. Thus, the basic sociological assumptions upon which affirmative action is based not only become articles of faith but they become bases for policies aimed at inhibiting the expression of opposition of any kind to the acceptance of those assumptions.

No one ever provides scientific evidence for this "hate" effect. No such evidence can be produced because human beings are not simply the result of external forces but how they respond to external forces. The real issue, I stress once more, is self-respect; self-respect is what comes from inside and cannot be given or taken away by anyone or anything external. What we are dealing with here are fundamentally conflicting notions of human nature.

Duplicity and hypocrisy have been introduced by affirmative action into the business world as well. Special bonuses are given by U.S. agencies to contractors who hire more minorities; whole contracts are given to minority contractors even when they do not have the lowest bid. One response is the growth and creation of contracting companies that have nominal minority owners and thereby qualify for these contracts. There is now also what Dinesh D'Souza calls a patronage industry for the civil rights establishment.[36]

Affirmative action leads to pervasive cynicism about American life. Consider the following statement by Gertrude Ezorsky:

> Whatever the effect of affirmative action measures in their entirety, it is true that racial preference for a less qualified black can, in specific situations, reduce effective job performance. . . . But the fact is that . . . hiring the most competent candidate is not the 'currently accepted' rule in employment. . . . Merit criteria are either ignored or undermined in several ways.[37]

What this says is that the world is not always fair, so there is nothing wrong with ignoring merit especially for a good cause like affirmative action. The trouble is that anyone can use this kind of argument to justify anything. When most citizens come to believe that there is no use to opposing injustice, the entire polity will collapse.

> Lies and deceptions 'in a good cause' are all too common, and nowhere more so than in political and legal doctrines that falsely sail under the flag of 'civil rights.' The perversions of the law by federal judges appointed for life have been especially brazen. While they may be personally immune to the outrage they create, neither the law nor respect for the law is immune. Courts receive

unprecedentedly low ratings in polls and contempt for the law is all too apparent in all too many ways. Demoralizing a people is not a small responsibility.[38]

Affirmative action, by promoting multiculturalism in a relativist sense, leads to nihilism and political fascism. Let me put this in the most forceful way. Affirmative action has led to the lowering of standards. In order to counteract this recognition, some advocates of affirmative action maintain that the very notion of standards is political. That is, they claim that there is no such thing as an objective standard—only different perspectives. For example:

> Deconstruction has been the theme of much speculation on the O.J. [Simpson] verdict. It has been claimed incessantly that black Americans on and off the jury 'saw' the evidence differently because they brought their own experiences (of police brutality, etc.) to the judgment. Since whites had a different experience, black and white 'truths' were different. And never the twain shall meet. All this is the greatest nonsense. It denies that there is such a thing as truth or objective reality. Indeed, it logically implies that Simpson could be both guilty and innocent of his wife's murder—depending upon who's reaching the verdict. But it is the identical argument used to justify 'diversity' in the newsrooms of mainstream press. As the diversity-mongers put it, we need black, Hispanic, lesbian, gay, etc. perspectives on the news.[39]

We cannot have it both ways. There cannot be the objective truth that there are different truths. If everything is a matter of perspective, then there is no reason to take anyone else's perspective seriously. Without shared values in a common perspective, tolerance and respect will evaporate to be replaced by the politics of fascism. Recall that the ultimate argument in favor of fascism is that since every one and every group is only out for itself, we need a strong and dictatorial leader to divide up the pie.

The perversion of critical thinking is most apparent in the case of affirmative action. Part of this perversion reflects what can only be identified as the insistence upon seeing everything from a group perspective. Jesse Jackson, for example, denies that there has been reverse discrimination, that "it is a myth that white males are being hurt." His evidence for this includes the statistic that White males are 33 percent of the population but 80 percent of the tenured professors.[40] Does this show that individual White males have not been passed over since the inception of affirmative action in favor of African American candidates? It does according to Jesse Jackson because the group of White males as a whole is doing as well or better than other groups! This kind of thinking marks the inability to conceptualize issues except in terms of group think.

The kind of thinking upon which affirmative action arguments thrive is an idiosyncratic one long popular in the social sciences. In legitimate scientific thinking we speculate on the hidden structure behind how things appear on the surface. If successful, we replace our ordinary understanding by appeal to previously hidden structures. The discoveries of atoms, viruses, and genes are examples. In imitation of the real sciences, the pseudo-social sciences attempt to explain social phenomena by appeal to hidden structures. Unlike legitimate physical science, the alleged hidden structures to which pseudo-social science appeals never get confirmed empirically. What we get is an unending series in which one faddish language replaces another. In the presence of competing theories of hidden structures, and with no way to choose among them, pseudo-social science resorts to the following technique. Instead of refuting alternative views, pseudo-social scientists speculate on the hidden structure behind the alternative views. That is, they speculate on why their adversaries hold what they take to be false views. In short, they give hidden structure accounts of alternative views of hidden structures. The end result is that instead of honest intellectual dialogue, they dismiss their opponents as victims of some hidden force. It is much easier to call your opponent a racist or sexist than to answer objections about the incoherence of affirmative action.[41] By the substitution of speculative hypotheses about the alleged underlying causes of our "corrupt" values, the kind of thinking stressed in the pseudo-social sciences is responsible for the demise of critical thinking.

The policy of affirmative action has put the nation in peril, according to R. Nieli.

> America must not think that it is automatically immune to the fate of these other lands. One simple fact is this: the principle of ethnic tribalism, if not counter-balanced by a more universal-human principle—such as that all men are created equal, that we are all part of the same *human* race, that in the eyes of God there is no Jew or Greek—is a principle of social chaos, and ultimately, a formula for civil war.[42]

The philosophy of non-violence of Dr. Martin Luther King, Jr. became a successful strategy because it appealed to the common moral conscience of America. It was precisely because that common moral conscience existed that people could be shamed. Do we now really want to undermine the very idea and content of the common moral core that made this possible?

Beyond Affirmative Action: A New Approach

Affirmative action consists of an overlapping series of policies intended to deal with the problem that African Americans do not fully participate in American life. Failure to participate fully means being overrepresented in prison populations and welfare recipiency.

> Blacks make up approximately 12 percent of the nation's population. Yet according to Uniform Crime Reports, published annually by the FBI, blacks account for 39 percent of those arrested for aggravated assault, 42 percent of those arrested for weapons possession, 43 percent of those arrested for rape, 55 per cent of those arrested for murder, and 61 per cent of those arrested for robbery. Even discounting for the possibility of some racial bias in criminal arrests, it seems clear that the average black person is between three and six times as likely to be arrested for a crime as the average white person. Young black males are arrested and convicted of crimes at an astonishingly high rate. According to the Sentencing Project, a liberal advocacy group, about 25 [we now know this figure to be 33 percent] percent of young black men in America are in prison, on probation, or on parole on any given day. . . . In major cities, the figures for young black men are even higher.[43]

No one disputes this statement. What is disputed is the interpretation or explanation of this set of symptoms. Given conflicting diagnoses, we shall end up with conflicting prescriptions for treatment.

For the past half-century, we have as a nation largely operated with a particular paradigm for diagnosing our social predicament. For the sake of argument, I shall identify the paradigm as the liberal paradigm.

The *liberal paradigm* makes the following assumptions:

(1) human beings are born with impulses that are basically good (a denial of the traditional Christian doctrine of original sin);

(2) all antisocial behavior is the result of external environmental influence (e.g., lack of information or resources, presence of hostile attitudes); and (3) in order to make people whole again, it is

necessary to engage in social engineering or the reconstruction of institutions so as to provide information and resources and to eliminate hostile attitudes.

The liberal paradigm was introduced as far back as the eighteenth century by a group of French *philosophes*, and this movement has become known as the Enlightenment Project. But it is only within the last half century that it has come to dominate public policy in the United States. It is now a pervasive view that totally dominates higher education (including law schools and think tanks) and all those affected by higher education. Entire political careers are fashioned on this paradigm since the point of being elected to political office is to propose and initiate innovative programs of social technology financed through tax dollars and overseen by governmental agencies.

Given this paradigm, how do people respond to the overrepresentation of African Americans and to their failure to participate fully in American life? Almost all antisocial behavior on the part of African Americans is excused as due to ignorance, poverty, and racism on the part the rest of the society. The suggested solution is more and better education (opposing segregated schools even when the resources available are the same, advocating busing, lowering admission standards so that African Americans can move more rapidly to the next educational level), increasing resources (higher welfare expenditure; raising the minimum wage; hiring, training, and promoting African Americans more rapidly than past performance warrants; contract set-asides; i.e., affirmative action), and eliminating or muting hostile attitudes toward African Americans (increasing contact among the races in schools and elsewhere, promoting role models, increasing the presence of African Americans in advertisements, producing a stream of works of literature and film that depict African Americans as victims, constantly reminding us that those who oppose these policies and the liberal paradigm in general are contributing to the hostile environment, constantly rehearsing public reaffirmations of solidarity with oppressed peoples, and supporting just about any program that is well intentioned or designed to put the liberal paradigm into practice no matter how flimsy the support). What is frequently identified as "liberal guilt" might be more aptly described as continual efforts to do something even in the face of the failure and counterproductivity of all previous efforts where the efforts reflect a commitment to the liberal paradigm.

The liberal paradigm is inadequate. It is inadequate, to begin with, because it does not work. As in the case of all paradigms when the evidence begins to mount against it there is a series of *ad hoc* changes designed to shore up the failing paradigm.[44] Affirmative action will be seen someday as just such an *ad hoc* policy.

One example of the failure of the liberal paradigm to explain overrepresentation adequately is the fact that African Americans who immigrated to the United States voluntarily from the West Indies have been remarkably successful despite facing the same obstacles as those who were descendants of slaves.[45] This clearly suggests that cultural attitudes are as important if not more important than environmental conditions.

But sooner or later the evidence becomes so massive that people begin to question the paradigm. We are now at the point where many well intentioned and intelligent people are willing to question the paradigm and not to vilify the messenger. It has become clear that until recently supporters of the liberal paradigm had become comfortable conformists in their thinking about social issues, too embarrassed to dissent, unable to acknowledge new facts and unwilling to rethink their prejudices.

It is a common observation that generals are always fighting the last war, and as in the case of the French building the Maginot line, the generals are unprepared for the new context. Stated in broader terms, the observation points to the extent to which certain early experiences are so formative of our thinking that we cannot recognize the existence of new circumstances. The First World War produced a kind of isolationism; many who lived through the Great Depression of the 1930s find a planned economy the only thinkable policy; many who experienced the Vietnam War are incapable of imagining a justifiable use of military force. In the same way, those who remember segregation in the South have come to adopt a rigid and outmoded model of explaining the problems that confront African Americans.

Is there an alternative paradigm for understanding the failure of African Americans as a group to participate fully in American life? There is an alternative, which I shall designate as the conservative paradigm.

The *conservative paradigm* makes the following assumptions: (1) human beings are born with self-destructive impulses as well as wholesome ones (i.e., an acceptance of the Christian doctrine of original sin with or without a theological framework); (2) anti-social behavior is the natural result of a lack of self-discipline; self-discipline is learned behavior but it is not totally induced from the outside, because while outside example and support is important, the final result depends upon free will; and (3) in order to make people whole, we must provide them not only with good examples (i.e., examples of self-discipline) but also with opportunities to learn in an internal sense self-control and personal responsibility by holding them responsible for what they do. This is not a political or technical task but a moral one.

Notice that the conservative paradigm does not deny the importance of environmental influence but it does stress that there is something more fundamental than the environment, namely human free will, and it has a different conception of what constitutes a benign environment. The conservative paradigm is not a call for inaction but for action; however, it denies that there is a guaranteed utopian resolution of the human predicament.

How do those who accept the conservative paradigm respond to the predicament of African Americans? Fundamental to the conservative paradigm is opposition to the rhetoric of victimization. This is not to deny past history or even its relevance, but rather to stress that what is most important is to take personal responsibility. The rhetoric of victimization (I call it "rhetoric" because it is not a hypothesis that has scientific support) seeks to explain what happens to African Americans totally in terms of larger social forces without due consideration to the moral response of individuals. Further, the conservative paradigm opposes granting special privileges (which is what affirmative action as preference is all about) precisely because you cannot learn self-discipline by having things made easier.

> the essential problem with this form of affirmative action is the way it leaps over the hard business of developing a formerly oppressed people to the point where they can achieve proportionate representation on their own (given equal opportunity) and goes straight for the proportionate representation. This may satisfy some whites of their innocence and some blacks of their power. But it does very little to truly uplift blacks. . . . The old sin is reaffirmed in a new guise.[46]

Self-respect, which is what African Americans need in order to participate fully, comes from the inside, it comes from what an individual does for himself or herself. Given what I have said about the historical connection between Christianity and individuality, it is no accident that the most stable institution among African Americans has been religion. Self-respect is not to be confused with self-esteem, which comes from the recognition of others, and it is not to be confused with either false bravado or delusions of grandeur. Ernest van den Haag notes,

> "Groups of Negroes may profit: Negroes as a group will suffer. Their self-image of inferiority to whites and of inadequacy will be reinforced. And the white's image of Negroes as inferior, as less well qualified for most things than whites, will be confirmed."[47]

Crucially important to the conservative paradigm is the role of families. The family is the central institution where we learn self-discipline, generally because it is within the family that a special bond of affection exists that allows for the self-disclosure that expresses the need for change so necessary for self-critique and self-discipline. Any public policy that undermines families, no matter how well intentioned, undercuts any attempt to provide the conditions within which African Americans can come to participate fully. Unfortunately, affirmative action is part and parcel of all those forms of social engineering that have as an inadvertent consequence the weakening of family life. The increasing threat to the family is its loss of function as more and more is taken over by public agencies who thus compete for the attention and esteem of children.

What alternative account does the conservative paradigm offer for the lack of success of so many African Americans?[48] The modern notion of individuality upon which our culture is based has classical roots and roots in Christianity, but its immediate specific historical genesis is in the Reformation and the Renaissance. What is also crucial for us to remember is that even within our own liberal culture going back as far as the Renaissance and the Reformation *many people have not made the transition to individuality.* There is a whole complicated history behind this but what is important is to recognize that the most serious problem within modern liberal societies is the presence of the failed or *incomplete individual.*[49] Being an incomplete individual is a state of mind. It is not directly correlated with income, intelligence, or how articulate you are. Some incomplete individuals are highly intelligent. Either unaware of or lacking faith in their ability to exercise self-discipline, the incomplete individual seeks escape into the collective identity of communities insulated from the challenge of opportunity. These are people focused on avoiding failure rather than on achieving success. Phenomenologically speaking, the incomplete individual can identify himself or herself by feelings of envy, resentment, self-distrust, victimization, and self-pity, in short, an inferiority complex.

What really inhibits these people is *not* a lack of opportunity, *not* a lack of political rights, and *not* a lack of resources but a character defect, a *moral inadequacy*. Having little or no sense of individuality, they are incapable of loving what is best in themselves; unable to love themselves, they are incapable of loving others; incapable of loving others, they cannot sustain life within the family; in fact, they find family life stultifying. What they substitute for love of self, others, and family is loyalty to a mythical community. Instead of an umpire, they want a leader, and they conceive of such leaders as protectors who relieve them of all responsibility. This is what makes their sense of community pathological.

The leadership of pathological communalism inevitably exploits the group in the interests of itself. What such groups end up with are leaders who are their mirror image: leaders who are themselves incomplete individuals and who seek to control others because they cannot control themselves, who seek the emasculation of autonomous individuals, who prize equality and not competition. Of course, the relationship of the leadership to the rest of the community remains hierarchical in a feudal sense. In place of a market economy and limited government, we get economic and political tyranny. For example, "Willie Brown recently encouraged students to, 'basically, just terrorize' Professor Glynn Custred, co-author of the California Civil Rights Initiative, which would outlaw state-sponsored affirmative action."[50]

Hate crimes can be explained using this same model. Hate crimes are crimes directed against an individual seen as a representative of a group. Such hate itself reflects pathological identification with one group and the conceptualization of the world as a conflict among groups. Racism, in this sense, is not the result of ignorance but reflects pathological group identification. It can be overcome only by promoting a sense of individual autonomy among all members of a society.

African Americans are not the only ones who exhibit the pathology of the incomplete individual, but they are the most visible. It is not slavery and discrimination that caused them to be incomplete individuals, for they were incomplete individuals before those events (a phenomenon I discuss below). Many others exhibit the same forms of pathological behavior under a variety of circumstances.

What do I mean by saying that African Americans were "incomplete individuals" before arriving in the United States? To begin with, only those who developed within the modern Western European tradition of liberal culture could even become individuals, in the sense of being autonomous and inner directed. For most of history and in most parts of the world, anonymity prevailed because people identified themselves by membership in some group. In Africa, the relevant locus of identification was and is the tribe.

What happens when a nonindividualist culture comes into contact with liberal culture, as for example in the transition from feudalism to capitalism, the advent of colonialism, the transition of former "iron curtain" countries or Third World communities to a market economy, or the current detribalization in Africa? A frequent result, as detailed by Oscar Lewis, is the culture of poverty.[51] The *culture of poverty* is marked by social, moral, and economic disintegration and perpetual dependence. So the second thing I mean by identifying African Americans as incomplete individuals is that given their background in Africa, it was to be expected that they would react to and adapt to their marginal position by developing a culture of poverty. It was not the slavery per se that led to the culture of poverty, but the meeting of two different worlds and the lack of resources within their prior world for adapting to the new world. This condition was perpetuated even after slavery was ended. The substitution of a new Afrocentrism to replace the emphasis of Dr. Martin Luther King, Jr., on the Christian (therefore Western European) dignity of humans as moral agents is a replay of the clash of cultures. Affirmative action is another adaptation to resist the development of the individuality for which Dr. King was striving.

Finally, another thing that contributed to (but did not cause) the perpetuation of the culture of poverty were government policies of segregation, paternalism, and most especially the dominance of the liberal paradigm. All of these failed to promote the sense of personal responsibility. I hasten to add that this factor is not a particular social structure but the failure to promote or encourage a change in psychological makeup; wherever individualism was allowed to flourish, many African Americans were able to participate to a remarkable degree despite public policies.

The question is not whether any of us will experience hostility in our lives but how we respond to the hostility, and how we respond reflects in part our sense of self. Nathan Glazer says, "some groups—even those bearing the badge of discrimination—have achieved more than equality. . . . To label [discrimination] as the cause of the economic differences between groups, even when it is extensive and pervasive, is a gross oversimplification."[52] I am not "blaming the victim" but calling attention to a different contextual explanation. But it is also true that the problem can never be solved by blaming the perpetrators of slavery or calling attention to conditions that no longer exist.

Consider the following analogy. Imagine an airplane with one hundred seats, fifty on each side of a center aisle. Imagine that forty of the passengers become violently ill on one flight. Imagine that of the ill passengers thirty are seated on the left side of the aisle and ten are seated on the right side of the aisle. Someone suggests that sitting on the left side of an airplane must cause a greater degree of motion sickness even though no engineering study can confirm this. On the other hand, someone else calls attention to the fact that the forty ill passengers chose the steak dinner while all of the other passengers chose the chicken dinner. Is it not more reasonable to suspect food poisoning than position on the aircraft? The proponents of affirmative action and supporters of the liberal paradigm are like those who keep calling attention to the fact that most of the sick people sat on the left side of the plane.

In an important sense, it no longer matters who is to blame. Blame is not the issue. The issue is how to solve the problem, and the problem can only be solved by promoting individuality. As Ralph Ellison reminds us: "Our task is that of making ourselves individuals. . . . We create the race by creating ourselves and then to our great astonishment we will have created a culture. Why waste time creating a conscience for something which doesn't exist? For you see, blood and skin do not think."[53]

What Can We Do?

There are seven actions that will remedy the present intolerable situation.

1. Stop using the expression 'affirmative action.' The term carries with it too much ambiguity, a legal and moral vacuousness, and assumptions about the underlying causes of social problems that are indefensible.
2. Stop making the liberal paradigm the only framework for the discus-

sion of public policy issues. Let us engage in an open and honest reappraisal of our problems.

3. Stop using terms like 'discrimination' and 'racism'so broadly that they cover whatever and whoever challenges the liberal paradigm.[54]

4. Stop condescending to African Americans—for their sake, and our sake, and also so that we do not undermine our polity by accepting the wrong conceptualization of public policy issues.

5. Outlaw affirmative action by legislation.[55] This is the only way to release business and other institutions from fear of litigation.

6. Challenge the liberal paradigm and challenge logical nonsense that emanates from anyone, including African Americans. Legitimate critique of African American irresponsibility as well as everyone else's.

7. Examine seriously the culpability of White liberal intellectuals in perpetuating an African American underclass both by holding the wrong moral, social, political, and economic analysis and by exploiting these people because of the rhetorical need to be able to point to an 'underclass'.[56] Ideas have consequences, including moral ones.

Of any social policy we may ask three questions: (1) Will it achieve its goal? (2) Is it the only way to achieve the goal? (3) Does it conflict with other goals? I assert that affirmative action cannot achieve the goal of overcoming "overrepresentation" because it is based on a misconception of the root of the problem. I assert that affirmative action is not the only way of dealing with "overrepresentation" in prisons and welfare, and I have outlined an alternative account here. Finally, I assert that affirmative action conflicts with every major norm in our culture. It is deeply illegal and immoral. It contributes to the serious undermining of the moral, social, economic, political, and legal order.

Notes

1. There are always interesting anomalies in statistical evidence. For example, African-American women college graduates on average earn more than White women college graduates (*The Economic Status of Black Women: An Exploratory Investigation*. [Washington, D.C.: U.S. Commission on Civil Rights, 1990], 12).

2. An obsession with 'success' understood in terms of prestige is symptomatic of the academic world, a world in which most of the literature on affirmative action is produced. See N. Capaldi, *Out of Order: Affirmative Action and the Crisis of Doctrinaire Liberalism*. Buffalo: Prometheus Books, 1985.

3. Charles Murray, *Losing Ground: American Social Policy, 1950-1980*. New York: Basic Books, 1984.

4. G. Horne, *Reversing Discrimination: The Case for Affirmative Action*. New York: International Publishers, 1992, 1.

5. See M. Rosenfeld, *Affirmative Action and Justice: A Philosophical and Constitutional Inquiry*. New Haven: Yale University Press, 1991, 47–48: "Affirmative action shall be assumed henceforth to include some kind of preferential treatment. Specifically, affirmative action shall refer to the preferential hiring, promotion, and laying off of minorities and women, to the preferential admission of minorities or women to universities, or to the preferential selection of businesses owned by minorities or women to perform government public contracting work for purposes of remedying a wrong or of increasing the proportion of minorities or women in the relevant labor force, entrepreneurial class, or university student population. Moreover, such preferential treatment may be required in order, among other things, to achieve a defined goal or to fill a set quota."

6. Humphrey (110 Cong. Rec. 12723).

7. Williams (110 Cong. Rec. 1433)

8. Clark (110 Cong. Rec. 7218)

9. Celler (110 Cong. Rec. 1518)

10. *Griggs v. Duke Power Co.*, 401 U.S. 424 (1971).

11. Powell, 1978, 2751, note #36, *Supreme Court Reporter*, 98A.

12. Controversial intervening cases included: (a) *United Steelworkers of America v. Weber* (1979). Under pressure from the Labor Department, Kaiser Aluminum and the United Steelworkers agreed to a training program which imposed a 50 percent quota for African Americans. The agreement was temporary; there was no commitment to maintaining racial balance; and no decision on defining what is permissible affirmative action. Most notable in this case is Justice Rehnquist's dissent in which he argued that even the "voluntary" policy is inconsistent with Title VII, and his critique of Justice Brennan in which Rehnquist denounced the idea that Title VII does not require but permits preference as an "Orwellian" interpretation of the law. (b) *Fullilove v. Klutznick* (1980). Here, the majority upheld minority set-asides as a version of our definition 2. (c) *Wygant v. Jackson Board of Education* (1986). The Board of Education of Jackson, Michigan, and the local teacher's union had entered into an agreement whereby layoffs were determined not simply by seniority but in order to maintain racial balance. The majority's view, as expressed by Justice Powell, reasserted that group classifications are suspect and justified only if they serve a compelling state interest and must be tailored so as not to burden innocent parties. (d) *Richmond v. Croson* (1989). The City of Richmond, Virginia, itself had adopted a 30 percent set-aside provision for minority contractors. Here the majority held that racial classifications are suspect categories.

13. O'Connor (1995, *Adarand*), 1839–41.

14. See L.D. Weeden, "Just Say No to Race Exclusive College Scholarships: From an Afrocentric Perspective," *Thurgood Marshall Law Review*, xx, 1995, 205–241.

15. Harlan, 163 U.S. 537, 16 S. Ct. 1146. See Charles A. Lofgren, *The Plessy Case: A Legal-Historical Interpretation.* New York: Oxford University Press, 1987.

16. 163 U.S. 537, 559 (1896) (Harlan, J., dissenting).

17. 163 U.S. 537, 1147.

18. Scalia (1995, *Adarand*) 1844.

19. Thomas (1995, *Adarand*) 1845.

20. Lincoln, 1864 address to 166th Ohio Regiment (1907), 206.

21. Califano quoted in P.C. Roberts and L.M. Stratton, "Proliferation of Privilege," *National Review* (November 6, 1995), 41. See L. Pojman, "The Moral Status of Affirmative Action," *Public Affairs Quarterly*, vi, 1992, 181–206.

22. Randy E. Barnett, "Compensation and Rights in the Liberal Conception of Justice," *Nomos*, xxxiii, 1991, 311–329, has made an even stronger case by pointing out that compensation in Anglo-American common law is tied to a liberal conception of justice that is rights-based not injury based. "In fact, the liberal conception of justice also requires that a right be violated before the legal system may justly rectify even a sharply defined injury produced by a discrete and unitary event clearly caused by a defendant's conduct." (315).

23. This Marxist analysis of the issue is to be found in Horne (1992), when he says "Affirmative action is necessary because of the past and present discrimination perpetrated primarily by a monopoly capitalist class that has sought to *profit* from the fruits of bigotry and to benefit politically from keeping the working class divided" (3).

24. G. Ezorsky, *Racism and Justice.* Ithaca, N.Y.: Cornell University Press, 1991, 35.

25. T. Sowell, "Are Quotas Good for Blacks?" in R. Nieli (ed.), *Racial Preference and Racial Justice.* Washington, D.C.: Ethics and Public Policy Center, 1991, 417.

26. L. Bowles, "Liberal Policies alienating Blacks," *Conservative Chronicle*, x, (November 1, 1995), 1.

27. See F. Hayek, *Road to Serfdom.* Chicago: University of Chicago Press, 1944, and F. Hayek, *The Fatal Conceit.* Chicago: University of Chicago Press, 1989.

28. For a devastating critique of the logic of egalitarianism, see S. Smilansky, "Nagel on the Grounds for Compensation," *Public Affairs Quarterly*, ix, 1995: "[Thomas] Nagel, and the main currents of egalitarian thought, have made life much too easy for themselves, in artificially limiting their perception of the grounds for compensation. . . . there is hardly any justification for this selective vision *in terms egalitarians can defend.* A consistent egalitarian must see the grounds for compensation in a very wide way, and this radically affects the acceptability of such a position" (72).

29. W.B. Allen, "Epstein's Challenge to the Civil Rights Regime," *San Diego Law Review*, xxxi, 1994, 57–66.

30. T. Machan, "Liberty and Racial Justice," *The Journal of Private Enterprise*, ix, (1993), 32–38. See also Terry Eastland, *Ending Affirmative Action: The Case for Colorblind Justice.* New York: Basic Books, 1996. Consult as well E.F. Paul,

F.D. Miller, J. Paul, and J. Ahrens (eds.), *Equal Opportunity*. Oxford: Basil Blackwell, 1987.

31. W. Williams, *State Against Blacks*. New York: McGraw-Hill, 1982.

32. Lani Guinier was nominated by President Clinton to be the U.S. Attorney General, but the furor created by her book *Tyranny of the Majority* (1994), led to the withdrawal of her nomination. In his review of that book, William Allen points out that Professor Guinier's views have not been mischaracterized in their essential thrust. What she said originally, and continues to say in the republished version, honestly and forthrightly proposes to abandon a vision of republican institutions in the United States, which may arguably be said to be a necessary ground of community in the society. According to Allen, "Guinier's Poetry of Race; or When Accepting the Reality of Difference Means Conceding Different Realities," *The Good Society*, v, 1995, "what grounds her [Guinier] moral claims is a view about community which delegitimizes the claims of the larger community in favor of the 'discrete and insular minority' " (36).

33. *National Review*, 6 November 1995, 6.

34. T. Sowell, *Race and Culture: A World View*. New York: Basic Books, 1994, 31.

35. For an illuminating discussion of this aspect of affirmative action see Stephen L. Carter, *Reflections of an Affirmative Action Baby*. New York: Basic Books, 1993.

36. Dinesh D'Souza, *The End of Racism*. New York: Free Press, 1995, pp. 317–322.

37. Ezorsky, *Racism and Justice*, 90.

38. T. Sowell, *Civil Rights: Rhetoric or Reality?* New York: William Morrow and Co., 1984, p. 120. See also L. Graglia, "The 'Remedy' Rationale for Requiring or Permitting Otherwise Prohibited Discrimination; How the Court Overcame the Constitution and the 1964 Civil Rights Act," *Suffolk University Law Review*, xxii, 1988, 569–621.

39. John O'Sullivan, "From the Editor," *National Review* (November 6, 1995), p. 4. See also R. Shalit, "Race in the Newsrooms," *New Republic* (October 2,1995), 20–37.

40. Jesse L. Jackson, "People of Color Need Affirmative Action," in A.E. Sadler (ed.), *Affirmative Action*. San Diego: Greenhaven Press, 1996, 9–10.

41. "It is apparent that the effort to point to affirmative action as a 'black program' and not what it is, i.e., a program designed to benefit the nation's majority, is just another effort to build on racial resentments backed by centuries of 'Afro-phobia' in order to hamper steps toward equality." Horne, *Reversing Discrimination*, 1.

42. Russell Nieli, "Ethnic Tribalism and Human Personhood," in R. Nieli (ed.), *Racial Preference and Racial Justice*, 103.

43. D. D'Souza, *The End of Racism*, 38–40.

44. C. Murray, *Losing Ground*.

45. T. Sowell, *The Economics and Politics of Race: An International Perspective*. New York: Quill, 1983.

46. Shelby Steele, *The Content of Our Character*. New York: St. Martin's Press, 1990, 115.

47. Ernest van den Haag, "Jews and Negroes," in R. Nieli (ed.), *Racial Preference and Racial Justice*, 391.

48. For a similar account with regard to women see Jennifer Roback, "Beyond Equality," *The Georgetown Law Journal*, lcccii, 1993, 121-133.

49. Michael Oakeshott, "The Role of the Masses in Representative Democracy," in T. Fuller (ed.) *Rationalism in Politics and Other Essays*. Indianapolis: Liberty Press, 1991, 363–383.

50. *National Review*, 6 November 1995, 8.

51. Oscar Lewis, *Five Families: Mexican Case Studies in the Culture of Poverty*. New York: Random House, 1959. See also Oscar Lewis, *La Vida*. New York: Random House, 1966.

52. Nathan Glazer, "Racial Quotas," in Nieli (ed.), *Racial Preference and Racial Justice*, 21.

53. Quoted in *The New Republic*, 6 November, 1995, 22.

54. Michael Levin, "Responses to Race Differences in Crime," *Journal of Social Philosophy*, xxiii, 1992, 5–29.

55. N. Lund, "Reforming Affirmative Action in Employment: How to Restore the Law of Equal Treatment." Committee Brief, No. 17 (2 August 1995). Washington, D.C.: The Heritage Foundation. A. Meyerson, "Nixon's Ghost: Racial Quotas—May They Rest in Peace," *Policy Review*, No. 73, 1995, 4–5.

56. S. Steele, "Affirmative Action Must Go," *New York Times* (1 March 1995):"affirmative action has always been. . . . iconographic public policy—policy that ostensibly exists to solve social problems but actually functions as an icon for the self-image people hope to gain by supporting the policy. From the beginning, affirmative action could be cited as evidence of White social virtue" (A15).

Response to Capaldi

Nicholas Capaldi presents affirmative action as a policy designed to solve the problem of the overrepresentation of African Americans among the unemployed and incarcerated. Defenders of affirmative action propose to accomplish this, he alleges, by reversing the underrepresentation of African Americans among the educated, employed, and successful. This, however, is a misrepresentation of the purpose of affirmative action, for it was not designed to address the plight of those who were not seeking employment or educational or investment opportunities. It was designed to provide qualified African Americans who were seeking such positions with increased possibilities of obtaining them by removing overt and institutional racist barriers.

At the time of the passage of the 1964 Civil Rights Act, the problem of the Black underclass was hardly recognized. Since that time, the gap between those who are most well off and those who are least well off has grown for both Whites and Blacks. Certainly, without affirmative action, many African Americans who are now educated, employed, and in productive positions would not be. But this is far from claiming that affirmative action was designed to solve the problems faced by those who are no longer seeking legitimate opportunities. It is a common ploy to portray affirmative action as having failed because it has not stemmed the growth of the least well off among African Americans. But this is to obscure the issue, for the ranks of the least well off continue to increase for everyone, not just for African Americans.[1]

Capaldi claims both backward-looking and forward-looking justifications of affirmative action are flawed because each assumes that African Americans who seek legitimate opportunities are disadvantaged by racism.

111

But, in his judgment, there is no objective evidence that racism is the cause of African Americans' disadvantages, and there is persuasive evidence that racism is not the cause.

Contrary to Capaldi's claim, there is no lack of evidence for the existence of racist barriers to African American participation in educational, employment, and investment opportunities. This evidence has been presented in a number of formats:

a. *Suits against major corporations and labor unions*: AT&T, Denny's, Shoney's, United Steelworkers of America, Sheet Metal Worker's International Union, Huntington Bancshares[2]

b. *Suits and public hearings involving governmental agencies*: Los Angeles Police Department, Detroit Police Department, New York Police Department, Philadelphia Police Department, the FBI, the Immigration and Naturalization Service, Miami Police Department, State Troopers of Alabama, New Jersey Department of Civil Service

c. *EEOC complaints*: documented cases of employment discrimination resulting from word-of-mouth recruitment and hiring/promotion decisions influenced by negative stereotypes.[3] Typical of recruitment discrimination is the recent settlement setting a target for the *New York Times* and the New York Newspaper Printing Pressmen's Union # 2 to hire 25 percent minorities and women over the next ten years. "The Consent decree affects free lance applicants who show up at the *Times'* Manhattan plant . . . applying to mop floors, clean printing machines, move stacks of compacted papers and perform other odd jobs. . . . In 1992 the union had no Blacks, Asians or women . . . and the casuals pool consisted entirely of White men, except for one person at the bottom of the list."[4]

d. *Carefully designed research studies*: studies showed that (a) retail car dealerships systematically offered substantially better prices on identical cars to White men than they did to Blacks and women; (b) when equally qualified Black and White candidates competed for a job, differential treatment, when it occurred, was three times more likely to favor the White applicant than the Black; and (c) baseball fans typically ascribed greater value to the cards of White players over the cards of Black players with similar play statistics (hits, doubles, triples, home runs, stolen bases, walks, etc).[5]

e. *Scientifically designed polls and surveys*: Polls by the National Opinion Research Center show that at the time of the passage of the 1964

Civil Rights Act, a majority of Whites objected to the idea of having a Black neighbor and believed that "White people should have the first chance at any kind of job."[6] Only fourteen years later, Harris polls indicated that less than 15 percent of Whites continued to openly endorse the view that Blacks were morally and intellectually inferior. Nonetheless, in a 1989 ABC News/*Washington Post* survey 25 percent of Blacks but only 4 percent of Whites believed that most Whites harbored covert racist views. Blacks in 1989 were two to three times more likely than Whites to believe Blacks were discriminated against in terms of housing, employment, and promotions.[7]

Polls and surveys have shown that a majority of both Blacks and Whites believe that any person can succeed with sufficient personal resolve and ability. Nonetheless, "the great majority of Blacks view discrimination as a major cause of the persisting Black-White gap" while a majority of Whites view the disparity as the result of Black lack of ability and determination.[8] While Blacks tend to attribute the cause of Black underachievement to situational factors beyond their own control, they tend to attribute Black achievements to personal talent and hard work. On the other hand, Whites tend to attribute Black underachievement to personal shortcomings and lack of effort on the part of Blacks, and Black achievements (as a group) to social interventions by the broader society.

Such biases among Blacks and Whites in the perception of racism and the explanation of Black inequality illustrate what cognitive psychologists call "attribution biases," whereby people tend to make causal attributions that cast themselves (and the group they identify with) in the most favorable light. Lee Sigelman and Susan Welch write:

> "Among Blacks, a group-serving bias would be consistent with blaming Whites or society in general for Blacks' problems while crediting Blacks for the progress they have made in recent years. Among White, a group-serving bias would be consistent with blaming Blacks for their problems and crediting Whites or society in general for the progress Blacks have made in recent years."[9]

Capaldi's failure to acknowledge the pervasive evidence for racism, despite the many different forms such evidence has taken, lends credence to the claim that, in terms of the existence and operation of racism, many Blacks and Whites occupy different perceptual worlds. The bias Capaldi exhibits in choosing his evidence is shown in his readiness to accept the success of West Indians as a counterexample to the central causal influence of racial discrimination, despite selective migration and numerous important disanalogies between the situations of West Indian and African Americans.[10]

Capaldi condemns affirmative action as immoral and offers in its place a conservative solution to the problem of African American participation in the opportunities of American life, which "accepts the traditional Christian doctrine of 'original sin' " and assumes that "human beings are born with self-destructive impulses."[11]

Such notions are reminiscent of seventeenth and eighteenth-century Christian accounts of the origin of races, in which Africans were the descendants of Ham. According to such accounts Shep, Ham, and Japheth were the sons of Noah, and each was viewed as a founder of one of the three major races. Ham is alleged to have broken the moral law by looking upon Noah naked. In medieval Talmudic commentaries, Ham is also alleged to have disobeyed Noah's rule against fornicating on the ark, thereby encouraging others to do the same and endangering the carrying capacity of the ark. For such infractions, God is supposed to have cursed Ham by decreeing that his descendants would be "servants of servants" to the progeny of Shem (the yellow race) and Japheth (the White race). The stereotype of the African as sexually promiscuous, socially irresponsible, and cognitively deficient continues this view.[12]

Capaldi rejects the argument that affirmative action is needed to overcome negative stereotypes such as this because, in his view, many beliefs about African Americans are not false stereotypes but true empirical generalizations. Thus, "feeling threatened by [African American] teenagers is not a matter of either prejudice or of stereotyping but a justifiable prudential reaction" given "the perceived failure of so many African Americans to embody fundamental values such as responsibility and civility." He cautions that "in dealing with strangers we have no recourse but to rely upon what common sense tells us."[13]

But this kind of reaction is exactly what is worse about prejudiced judgments based on unexamined stereotypes. Because it ignores a host of relevant questions such as: Are all African American teenagers to be judged as if they are "essentially" like those charged with breaking the law? Are those charged with breaking the law victims of selective enforcement? Are the laws themselves designed so that they have a disparate impact on African Americans?[14] Research in cognitive psychology has shown that "commonsense" generalizations are often made on the basis of samples chosen because they are vivid and easily recalled. Judgments made on the basis of such generalizations are typically accepted uncritically and exhibit many common fallacies.

The point of antidiscrimination laws is to prohibit imputing stereotypical characteristics to individuals that exclude them from opportunities they are qualified for. Antidiscrimination laws force us not to "rely on what common sense tells us," in recognition of the many errors typical of common sense judgements.[15] Until we have instituted the habit of examining stereotypical claims critically, it is quite likely that "traditional Christian" and other commonsensical accounts of African American underachievement will appear as plausible as accounts based on carefully established fact.

It is paradoxical that Capaldi would endorse evaluating individuals in terms descriptive of their group. That a high proportion of African American men between fourteen and twenty-eight are involved with the legal system is a fact about the group that involves no necessary implication about any particular African-American teenager. To prejudge a person on the basis of popular beliefs about that person's group is exactly what Capaldi has said we should not do. Indeed, it is precisely because of the prevalence and persistence of such prejudgments in the history of this country that discrimination on the basis of race and sex is unlawful.

Responses to survey research questions indicate that negative stereotypes of Blacks as lazy, undisciplined, and prone to criminal activity are still quite common among Whites and are highly correlated with opposition to race-based measures such as affirmative action. To the extent that Blacks are seen as responsible for their situation because of lack of effort and discipline, to that extent are Blacks seen as undeserving of any kind of special consideration.[16]

For Capaldi, African-American antisocial behavior is the result of lack of self-discipline and internal self control. Because, he argues, many African Americans are "unable to love themselves, they are incapable of loving others." They feel inferior and have a sense of identify only by identifying with some larger group so that success by any member of the group is vicarious success for each individual.[17] Capaldi writes:

> African Americans are not the only ones who exhibit the pathology of the incomplete individual, but they are the most visible. It is not slavery and

discrimination that caused them to be incomplete individuals, for they were incomplete individuals before those events; many others exhibit the same forms of pathological behavior under a variety of circumstances.[18]

Capaldi claims that Africans were "incomplete individuals" prior to the impact of the slave trade because they identified with tribal affiliations. However, most immigrants that have come to the United States have identified themselves in terms of ethnic and religious affiliations.[19] What distinguishes African Americans from other American ethnic groups is the fact that slavery was designed to produce "incomplete individuals."

While John Locke is known for his advocacy of the inalienable right of each individual to the fruits of his or her labor, he did not extend this right to the African slave in America. Rather, Locke supported slavery on the grounds that African slaves were captives of war who would have been put to death were it not for the slave trade. He held that their sentence of death was commuted in favor of a form of *social death*. The slave was physically alive, but from the point of view of the dominant society, the slave as an autonomous person was dead and had no rights that need be respected by a freeman.[20]

Whippings were used not merely to punish slaves for doing something wrong, but also to impress upon them that they were slaves, and subject to the whims of their masters. In a similar way, slave women were subject to the carnal desires of their masters, and no freeman could be convicted of the rape of a slave woman. The slave was forced to internalize the master's right to domination, accept servitude as a duty, and adopt the master's point of view as his or her own.

It is difficult to see how Capaldi could ignore the role of slavery and segregation in shaping the personality of any African Americans that might fit his description of "incomplete individuals." It is also difficult to see how Capaldi could ignore all the African Americans who do not fit that description. Nonetheless, he maintains that "we are not 'blaming the victim' but calling attention to a different contextual explanation."[21] And from the point of view of that explanation, "affirmative action cannot achieve the goal of overcoming 'overrepresentation' because it is based on a misconception of the root of the problem."[22] Not only does Capaldi misrepresent the goal of affirmative action, he clearly suggests that Africans have some kind of constitutional deficiency that has carried over to African Americans. It is amazing that he offers no serious defense of this claim.

I will observe the spirit of charity and interpret Capaldi's views in light of his commitment to the conservative cause. Whatever the cause of African American marginality in American life, perhaps his aversion to increased governmental intervention in private decisions is the primary reason for his opposition to affirmative action. This would accord with his suggestion that the correct solution for all (or most) of our social problems is an unrestricted market.

Following Tibor Machan, Capaldi recommends "that private individuals and organizations be allowed to discriminate but only if that is their publicly announced policy. [Otherwise] . . . discrimination should be illegal only if practiced by government."[23] Capaldi's motivation in allowing private discrimination is not to reintroduce the historic advantages Whites have had in competition with Blacks. Rather, "the presumption behind this suggestion is that between general public revulsion and the workings of the market private discriminators would not be able to compete."[24]

There is good reason to believe, however, that Capaldi's presumption might not hold, and that the market might find it less costly and more efficient *not* to correct for injuries of racial prejudice imposed on Blacks. I have argued that in a slack market where there is a surplus of skilled labor it is rational to continue to discriminate. Under such conditions, conservatives and liberals alike have acknowledged that inequities introduced in the past would tend to be preserved rather than eliminated by the market.[25] Given this prospect, the question is whether market efficiency is to take precedence over social justice.

It is difficult to see how Capaldi can insist on the detrimental effect of big government on personal autonomy while denying the detrimental effect of socially sanctioned racial prejudice on the personal autonomy of African Americans. Implicit even in the conservative paradigm is the recognition that certain external conditions must be satisfied in order for individuals to exercise their internal capacity for freedom.[26]

One of these conditions is the equal opportunity to accumulate wealth. For Capaldi, wealth is good because it is a means to achieve one's goals, and it liberates us from the culture of poverty, it enhances individual liberty, checks governmental power, and provides the dynamic of social reform.[27] Most people save to benefit their children as much as themselves. Indeed, the tendency for wealth and poverty to be inherited is one of the strongest research findings in social science.[28] As much as two-thirds of the variation in the success of succeeding generations is accounted for by the intergenerational transfer of assets and "approximately half of all great wealth is inherited."[29]

Clearly, "wealth generates power, and power generates privileges conducive to accumulation of still greater wealth."[30] But frugality and hard work matter little if barriers are allowed that systematically exclude certain groups from opportunities available to others. Both statistical disparities and survey research indicate that Whites are prone to deny Blacks benefits and services they would make available to other groups. This "racial double standard," whether it be overt or covert, is a form of racism that has acted to depress the accumulation of assets in the Black community.[31] The principle purpose of affirmative action policies is to identify and neutralize barriers that limit African Americans' access to opportunities for the accumulation of human skills, real property, and financial assets. To approve of government efforts to enhance the acquisition of such forms of wealth for European Americans but deny such efforts in the case of African Americans is racist, whatever the intent.

Notes

1. My thanks to Sam Hunter for this point.

2. Huntington Mortgage Co., a subsidiary of Huntington Bancshares, was found to charge higher fees to black mortgage applicants than to white applicants. *New York Times*, 19 October, 1995. Shoney's paid 132 million in 1992 to settle racial discrimination lawsuits filed by former employees. *New York Times*, 26 July, 1995.

3. See study by Jomills Braddock II and James McPartland, "How Minorities Continue to be Excluded from Equal Employment Opportunities: Research on Labor Market and Institutional Barriers," *Journal of Social Issues* 5 (1987): 43; Maurice Munroe, "The EEOC: Pattern and Practice Imperfect," *Yale Law & Policy Review*, 13, no.2, (1995): 219–79.

4. *New York Times*, 30 March, 1995, 6b.

5. (a) Ian Ayres, "Fair Driving: Gender and Race Discrimination in Retail Car Negotiations," *Harvard Law Review* 104, no.4 (February 1991): 817–72; (b) Margery Turner, Michael Fix, and Raymond Struyk, *Opportunities Denied, Opportunities Diminished: Racial Discrimination in Hiring*, (Washington, D.C.: The Urban Institute Press, 1991): 2; (c) Clark Nardinelli and Curtis Simon, "Customer Racial Discrimination in the Market for Memorabilia: The Case of Baseball" in *Quarterly Journal of Economics*, 105, no.3 (August 1990): 575–95.

6. Lee Sigelman and Susan Welch, *Black Americans' Views of Racial Inequality: The Dream Deferred* (New York: Cambridge University Press, 1991), 48–49.

7. Sigelman and Welch, *Black Americans' Views of Racial Equality* , 52–53.

8. Sigelman and Welch, *Black Americans' Views of Racial Equality* , 90–93.

9. Sigelman and Welch, *Black Americans' Views of Racial Equality*, 97.

10. For a comparison of the cases of West Indians and American Blacks, see chap. 5 of *The Politics of Racial Inequality* by J. Owens Smith (New York: Greenwood Press, 1987).

11. Capaldi, 99

12. Winthrop Jordan, *White over Black: American Attitudes toward the Negro, 1550–1812* (New York: Norton, 1977), 17–18, 35–37.

13. Capaldi, 83

14. While Blacks and Whites use illegal drugs at approximately the same rate, Blacks are arrested nearly five times as often as White youths. While crack cocaine is made from powder cocaine, the penalty for possession of 5 grams of crack is the same as that for possession of 500 grams of powder cocaine. The result has been long sentences for Blacks from the inner cities where crack is common and lenient treatment for suburban Whites who are more likely to use powder. A number of federal judges have protested this disparity in prosecution and sentencing, and the issue is now before the Supreme Court. See *New York Times*, 31 October 1995,18 and *New York Times*, 5 November 1995, 14; *Christian Science Monitor*, 1 March 1996, 3

15. See Richard Nisbett and Lee Ross, *Human Inference: Strategies and Shortcomings of Social Judgement* (Englewood Cliffs, N.J.: Prentice Hall, 1980).

16. See Paul Sniderman and Thomas Piazza, *The Scar of Race* (Cambridge, Mass: Harvard University Press, 1993).

17. Capaldi, 102.

18. Capaldi, 102–103; Presumably these "many others" include women, who are typically considered to be more concerned about their families than about their personal achievements.

19. The most successful of contemporary capitalists, the Japanese, are still known for the extent to which they exalt group over individual considerations.

20. See Orlando Patterson, *Slavery and Social Death* (Cambridge, Mass.: Harvard University Press, 1982).

21. Capaldi, 103—104.

22. Capaldi, 105.

23. Capaldi, 90.

24. Capaldi, 91.

25. Glenn Loury, "Why Should We Care about Group Inequality?" in *Social Philosophy and Policy* 5, no.1 (1988); Cass Sunstein, "Why Markets Don't Stop Discrimination" in *Reassessing Civil Rights*, ed. Ellen Frankel Paul, Fred Miller, Jr., and Jeffrey Paul (New York: Blackwell, 1991); Richard Epstein, *Forbidden Grounds* (Cambridge, Mass: Harvard University Press, 1992), chap.3.

26. See Immanuel Kant, "What Is Enlightenment" in *Kant Selections* ed. Lewis White Beck (New York: Macmillan, 1988), 462–467.

27. Capaldi, 75–76.

28. Michael Sherraden, *Assets and the Poor: A New American Welfare Policy* (New York: Sharpe, 1991), 121 .

29. Lester Thurow, *Generating Inequality* (New York: Basic Books, 1975), 197.

30. Sherraden, *Assets*, 126.

31. Sniderman and Piazza, *Scar*, 79.

Response to Mosley

Overview

With regard to Mosley's historical analysis, I have two general observations. First, Mosley locates affirmative action within the broader and more legitimate context of the Civil Rights tradition. This is a mistaken analysis, for affirmative action is antithetical to that tradition. The relevant legislation makes this clear, and the legislative history (e.g., Senator Humphrey's offer to eat every printed page of the Civil Rights Act of 1964 if quotas were to be found within it) makes it even clearer. I would like to have said the "civil rights movement," but this expression has become something very different since the death of Dr. Martin Luther King, Jr. Affirmative action goes beyond civil rights in encouraging an active policy of promoting something; but more important, what it is designed to promote is not freedom or excellence or meritocracy but proportionality. An important part of the story is the existence of many prominent individuals and organizations who fought discrimination but who came to distance themselves from the civil rights movement when the latter in its pursuit of proportionality embraced reverse discrimination. Affirmative action is not and never has been a policy in favor of equality of opportunity; its aim has always been equality of outcome.

Second, Mosley's assertion that the "clear intent" of the Act was to "redistribute opportunities" is patently false. Turning to Mosley's defense of affirmative action, I have eleven objections.

1. It is not entirely clear why we should accept either the backward-looking or the forward-looking arguments. After summarizing each, he engages in a rebuttal of the various objections they face. However, he begins this rebuttal without giving a comprehensive

or clear argument for why we should accept them in the first place. A sound argument must include a positive as well as a negative element.

2. Mosley's rebuttal of the charge of reverse discrimination misses the point. He claims that White males are not being denied benefits that they deserve but rather are being denied benefits that are the ill-procured product of slavery and discrimination. However, the point is not that White males are being denied benefits but that affirmative action denies them the opportunity to compete on an equal basis with other individuals. It does not matter that reverse discrimination, unlike Jim Crow laws, is intended to help African Americans and not to harm Whites. The consequence, however intended, of reverse discrimination is to deny Whites the full opportunity to compete.

3. Mosley's rebuttal of the argument that contemporary Whites should not be penalized for something they had no control over is equally unsatisfying. His rebuttal rests on the false assumption that the success of White individuals is the result of present discrimination.

4. Mosley's argument rests upon the assumption that pervasive discrimination still exists in American society and that it is this discrimination that is largely if not exclusively responsible for the gap in African-American achievement. Neither he nor anyone else ever provides evidence to support this assumption. Nor does he explain why the achievement of groups should be measured or measured against other groups.

5. Mosley's defense is based on the counterfactual argument that all races would be represented proportionately were it not for racism and discrimination, and that disproportional representation is evidence of racism. As I pointed out in my presentation, this is both an unfounded and circular argument.

6. Mosley argues that affirmative action is necessary to declare that "racial discrimination is no longer the order of the day." On the contrary, there are many ways of communicating this message that are less offensive, more just, and more effective.

7. Mosley never really provides a satisfactory answer to the alternative counterfactual argument that African Americans are actually better off now than they would have been without slavery (e.g., they

would be living in impoverished African dictatorships). Rather than respond directly to the argument, he skirts it. For example, he points out that in the absence of slavery present African Americans would not exist for the enslaved Africans would have reproduced differently. However, if we cannot in principle compare these two groups then the original counterfactual claim that the descendants of slaves have been harmed becomes incoherent.

8. I challenge Mosley's claim that the market would allow the problem to persist indefinitely into the future. Historical evidence (e.g., that compiled by Sowell and Williams) suggests exactly the opposite.

9. Mosley's assertion that the burden of proof should rest with the defendant in discrimination cases (and the opponents of affirmative action in general) goes against the grain of American justice, which is predicated on the belief of innocence until guilt is proven.

10. Mosley makes a curious statement about the need for African American professionals in African American communities. He writes, "this suggests that sociocultural factors such as language, physical identity, personal background and experiences are relevant factors in determining the kinds of communities in which a physician will establish a practice." If this is acceptable in the above context, why is it unacceptable for White CEOs to hire only White employees? This looks like a contradiction.

11. Mosley's defense of affirmative action is predicated on the existence of certain "barriers" that exclude African Americans from participating fully. Yet, he never identifies these mysterious barriers. Much less does he demonstrate that they do in fact impede the participation of African Americans.

Bureaucratic History and Judicial Myth

We have to distinguish among (1) what the first use of "affirmative action" meant, (2) the history of the expression "affirmative action," (3) how certain elements of the federal bureaucracy (specifically EEOC and HEW) interpreted and attached that expression to the Civil Rights Act of 1964, and (4) the arguments used to support (3). There are two reasons why we have to make these distinctions. The first is that most people do not know the real story. The myths that surround the story of affirmative action have clouded people's perception of the issues involved. The second reason is that the real story of affirmative action reveals a pervasive and deliberate misrepresentation of the law. As we shall see, the fourth (compensation) and fifth (preference) conceptions of affirmative action are figments of bureaucratic imagination.

Professor Mosley's first section is entitled "Legislative and Judicial Background," but the story he tells begins with an executive order. While there is a legislative and judicial background, the real story of affirmative action is a story largely centered around the federal bureaucracy operating in direct opposition to Congress and to the U.S. Supreme Court.

The expression "affirmative action" makes its first appearance in President Lyndon Johnson's Executive Order No. 11246 in 1965. An executive order is neither legislative nor judicial. Moreover, Johnson did not in that order define what the expression meant. In 1961, President Kennedy used the expression "affirmative steps" in his Order No. 10925 to direct contractors doing business with the federal government to recruit and encourage minority participation actively.

In May of 1968 the Department of Labor (another element of the executive bureaucracy) defined affirmative action in Order No. 4, which for the first time spoke of "an analysis of minority group representation" as well as "specific goals and timetables for the prompt achievement of full and equal employment opportunity."[1] Additional guidelines were issued on 5 February 1970. Affirmative action was further defined as "a set of specific and result-oriented procedures to which a contractor commits himself to apply every good faith." Finally, the guidelines issued on 4 December 1971 spelled out the ultimate logic of the policy. It turned on the concept of "underutilization":

> "underutilization" is defined as having fewer minorities or women in a particular job classification than would reasonably be expected by their availability.[2] The remedy is to place "eligible minority members in the position which the minority would have enjoyed if it had not been the victim of discrimination."[3]

What we see in this is the evolution of "affirmative action" within the executive branch of the government, specifically in the Department of Labor as well as EEOC (Equal Employment Opportunity Commission) and HEW (Health, Education, and Welfare). The evolution is from affirmative action as the open search to affirmative action as compensation (my previous definition 4) and as preference (definition 5). I stress that there is no basis for this evolution in the Constitution, or in previous legislation, or in the decisions of the U.S. Supreme Court. It is a pure bureaucratic fabrication emanating from staffers who were not elected but appointed, who did not and do not represent a cross section of America, and who consist largely of attorneys who are minorities and women committed to the liberal paradigm of public policy in opposition to the Constitution, to prior legislation, and to the decisions of the U.S. Supreme Court.

The explicit repudiation of affirmative action as compensation because it is in direct conflict with Titles VI and VII of the Civil Rights Act of 1964 (as Justice Rehnquist maintained) and in conflict with the Constitution as well as logically incoherent (as Justice Powell maintained) emerges in the *Bakke* (1978) case.

Supporters of affirmative action as compensation subsequently took comfort in the decision of the Court in the 1979 case of *Kaiser Aluminum & Chemical Corporation and United SteelWorkers of America, AFL-CIO v. Brian F. Weber.* Under pressure from the Labor Department overseeing a government contract, Kaiser and the Steelworkers union "voluntarily" agreed to establish a training program in which 50 percent of the participants would be minority workers and in which seniority would not count. Justices Powell and Stevens (who had supported *Bakke*) withdrew from the case. The Court upheld the training program because it was "voluntary." Various arguments instead of a consensus were offered in support of this decision. Brennan (who had opposed *Bakke*), for example, claimed that while Title VII did not require quotas it also did not forbid them! Stewart offered different arguments so as not to compromise his position in *Bakke*. Rehnquist, on the other hand, characterized Brennan's interpretation of Title VII as "Orwellian."

The *Weber* case turned out not to be as useful as supporters of affirmative action thought it would be. The *Weber* decision did not cover new jobs; the agreement was temporary; there was no commitment to racial balance; and no decision defining permissible affirmative action. With the addition of Justices Scalia, O'Connor, and Thomas, the Brennan interpretation faded from the scene. Finally, the *Adarand* case made clear that racial classifications must pass the test of strict scrutiny, that is, they must serve a compelling government interest and the remedy must be narrowly tailored to achieve that goal. As I have maintained in my original presentation, the *Adarand* case strictly limits affirmative action to the open search (definition 1) and punitive action (definition 2). Compensation (definition 4) is once more rejected, and preference (definition 5) never had a judicial life.

A second long-standing myth is the belief that Justice Powell's use of the concept of "diversity" in the *Bakke* case was the basis for affirmative action as preference. Justice Powell always maintained that any racial classification m st meet the test of strict scrutiny. At the same time, he also asserted that attaining a diverse student body is "a constitutionally permissible goal for an institution of higher education" because the diversity of viewpoints furthers academic freedom. However, Powell also insisted that ethnicity was "one element in a range of factors a university properly may consider in attaining the goal of a heterogeneous student body" and that "race or ethnic background may be deemed a 'plus' in a particular applicant's file, yet does not insulate the individual from comparison with all the other candidates for the available seats."[4]

Even if Powell's conception of diversity were generally accepted, it is important to see that it is (1) limited to universities, (2) not clear on how it applies to graduate programs, (3) applies to students not to faculty hiring, and (4) with regard to students does not permit quotas, set-asides, or separate admissions tracks. Scalia, for one, has even challenged its applicability to graduate programs. Although academic freedom may be a compelling interest, nowhere does Powell say that diversity is a compelling interest. Nor does Powell maintain that being of a certain race automatically presumes that the individual in question has either a unique or desirable perspective worthy of inclusion. All of this is precisely why Justices Brennan, White, Marshall, and Blackmun (all of whom opposed *Bakke*) implicitly rejected Powell's position. So the relatively weak use of the concept of "diversity" appeared only once in a Court decision and then only in the opinion of one justice. There is no logical road from Powell's position to preference, and subsequent Court case law suggests strongly that the state has no compelling interest in diversity that would justify race-based discrimination.

Important recent confirmation of this is to be found in *Hopwood v. State of Texas* (1996) in the Federal Fifth Circuit Court of Appeals. The law school at the University of Texas used different criteria and different subcommittees for reviewing applications by African Americans and Mexican Americans. Four White students sued the university on the grounds that they were denied admission because of the unlawful race-based policy. One of these students, Cheryl Hopwood, had outstanding credentials, is married to a U.S. serviceman, and has a child who is severely handicapped. The district court ruled in their favor, noting that the University of Texas Law School had violated their equal protection rights. This decision was upheld in even stronger terms in the Federal Appeals Court.[5]

In its own defense, the University of Texas, which has not practiced discrimination, argued that since the primary and secondary schools in the State of Texas had discriminated in the past, and since the University is also part of the State, it is legitimate for the University to remedy that discrimination. Further, it argued by appeal to the concept of diversity. It never made clear how these two arguments go together.

In his decision for Hopwood and against Texas, Circuit Judge Jerry E. Smith, noted the following:

1. Plaintiffs (Hopwood, etc.) did have their equal protection rights violated for the central purpose of that clause "is to prevent the States from purposefully discriminating between individuals on the basis of race," citing *Shaw v. Reno* (1993).
2. Discriminating by race is highly suspect and must pass the strict scrutiny test, citing, among other things, *Adarand* (1995).
3. "[The] consideration of race or ethnicity by the law school for the purpose of achieving a diverse student body is not a compelling interest under the Fourteenth Amendment." Moreover, "diversity fosters, rather than minimizes, the use of race. It treated minorities as a group, rather than as individuals . . . [and it] just as likely, may promote improper racial stereotypes, thus fueling racial hostility." Judge Smith also cites Richard Posner's 1974 DeFunis remark that "the use of a racial characteristic to establish a presumption that the individual also possesses other, and socially relevant characteristics, exemplifies, encourages, and legitimizes the mode of thought and behavior that underlies most prejudice and bigotry in modern America."
4. With regard to the claim that the University of Texas is responsible for rectifying earlier discrimination practiced by other schools in the

State, Judge Smith, citing *Wygant* and *Croson*, rejected it. "The state's use of remedial racial classifications is limited to the harm caused by a specific state actor." That is, affirmative action as punitive (definition 2) must be limited to an identifiable perpetrator, otherwise there is "no viable limiting principle." In our words, punitive action is not to be extended into amorphous compensation.

I doubt that this is the end of the story except in the logical sense. Proponents of affirmative action will continue to fabricate judicial myth until affirmative action is directly outlawed.

The history of "affirmative action" shows the following:

1. It confirms my original contention that the only legally acceptable meanings encompass the open search (definition 1) and punitive action (definition 2) limited to provable cases of discrimination and where numerical remedies are strictly limited to preserve the violation of rights.
2. Set-asides (definition 3) have been reduced to punitive action (definition 2) and must involve strict scrutiny.
3. Compensation and Preference have always been considered illegal by the Court!
4. No legislative body has ever passed a law embodying compensation or preference. Given popular opinion, it is ludicrous to suggest that there is any legislative basis for compensation or preference.
5. Supporters of affirmative action as compensation or preference have chosen to pursue their case within government bureaucracies and in the courts precisely because they recognize point four above, namely popular opposition. They have tried to get through the Court what they could never get through Congress.
6. Supporters of affirmative action had looked to activist justices (e.g., Marshall, Brennan, and Blackmun) to help them achieve judicially what could not otherwise be achieved. These justices were activist in the sense of adopting the liberal paradigm of public policy in such a manner as to undermine or overrule the moral and metaphysical foundations of the Constitution.

Although I recognize that justices may and do differ on their interpretation of the law, especially in applying old law to novel circumstances, I also recognize that there are serious philosophical differences that inform these disagreements. In identifying Marshall, Brennan, and Blackmun as activist I claim that the philosophical position of these justices allows them to disregard certain moral principles and traditional practices in the light of a set of sociological principles that are extraneous to the law and highly controversial if not down right false. We think Justice Brennan's reasoning in *Weber* is a particularly egregious example of this kind of thinking. A departure from sound principle in law is always advocated on the ground that it is entirely exceptional, strictly limited in its application, certain to do no harm, and intended to secure some great practical good. Unfortunately, once accepted it becomes a precedent for even further departures.

Linking compensation with preference in this fashion tries to combine two bad arguments in the hope of producing one good one. Preference becomes a substitute for compensation because compensation cannot stand on its own; and compensation becomes the rhetorical mask for preference because preference becomes in practice an odious quota system. This combination recognizes that although African Americans were victimized in the past current African Americans cannot be compensated for it under our conception of law (i.e., it is admitted that the first possibility is untenable, namely, the compensation argument on its own). Hence we subscribe to a system of preference in which some current African Americans are rewarded as a proxy for the injustices of the past. The advantage of this rhetorical linkage of the two arguments is that it relieves one of the burden of proving just exactly how current African Americans have been harmed by the past (something that is never shown), and it assuages the conscience of those African Americans who are the beneficiaries of the privileges of preference.

The foregoing argument is not a legal argument, for the law does not recognize the conception of compensation to which the argument appeals; it is not a moral argument, for it asks us to suspend our traditional moral beliefs. It is a political argument. Our critique of this linkage argument has been to stress how antithetical it is to fundamental American values to conceptualize social policy in this fashion.

Notes

1. Order No. 4 (Title 41, C.F.R., 60–1.40).
2. Underutilization (41, C.F.R., 60–2.11).

3. U.S. Commission on Civil Rights, *Statement on Affirmative Action*, October 1977, 7–8. This is a quote from *Rios v. Steamfitters Local 608*, 501 F.2d at 631–32.

4. *Bakke*, 438 U.S. 311–316 (1978).

5. 1996 WL 120235 (5th Cir. (Tex)).

Index

About the Authors

Albert G. Mosley is professor of philosophy at Ohio University. He is the editor of *African Philosophy: Selected Readings* and numerous articles on affirmative action.

Nicholas Capaldi is McFarlin Professor of Philosophy at the University of Tulsa. Among his books is *Out of Order: Affirmative Action and the Crisis of Doctrinaire Liberalism.*